JUMBLE® Sensation

The Puzzles that are Sweeping the Nation!

Henri Arnold, Bob Lee, Jeff Knurek, and Mike Argirion

TRIUMPH
BOOKS

This book is available in quantity at special discounts
for your group or organization.

For further information, contact:

Triumph Books
542 South Dearborn Street
Suite 750
Chicago, Illinois 60605
(312) 939-3330
Fax (312) 663-3557
www.triumphbooks.com

Printed in U.S.A.

ISBN: 978-1-60078-548-1

Design by Sue Knopf

Contents

JUMBLE®

Sensation

Classic Puzzles

JUMBLE®

Unscramble these four Jumbles, one letter to
each square, to form four ordinary words.

SYTUL

SOUMY

FLYNUK

FRIDAT

WHAT THE NEWLY-
WEDS CONSIDERED
THEIR CHECKING
ACCOUNT.

Now arrange the circled letters to form the
surprise answer, as suggested by the above
cartoon.

*Print
answer* **A**
here

JUMBLE®

Unscramble these four Jumbles, one letter to
each square, to form four ordinary words.

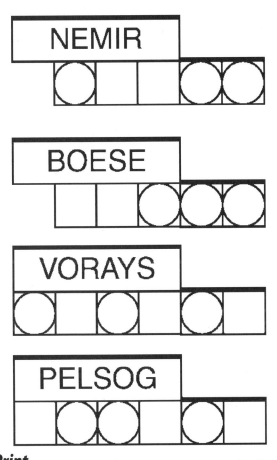

NEMIR

BOESE

VORAYS

PELSOG

Put it in
gear. No,
not backward

CRASH!

Oops!

LEARNING HOW TO
DRIVE CAN LEAD
TO THIS.

Now arrange the circled letters to form the
surprise answer, as suggested by the above
cartoon.

*Print
answer
here*

"   "

JUMBLE®

Unscramble these four Jumbles, one letter to each square, to form four ordinary words.

FOIMT

IMODI

ENBODY

SAYNUE

Go ahead. Ask me anything

We're ready for the test

WHEN THE ROOM-
MATES STUDIED
ANATOMY, THEY
KNEW THEIR
SUBJECT——

Now arrange the circled letters to form the surprise answer, as suggested by the above cartoon.

Print answer here

JUMBLE®

Unscramble these four Jumbles, one letter to each square, to form four ordinary words.

PHAMC

DUTIA

CULTOC

GLOANS

How 'bout dinner tonight?

SHE DECIDED TO GO OUT WITH THE OUTFIELDER BECAUSE HE WAS----

Now arrange the circled letters to form the surprise answer, as suggested by the above cartoon.

Print answer here A ⬡⬡⬡⬡ " ⬡⬡⬡⬡⬡ "

JUMBLE®

Unscramble these four Jumbles, one letter to each square, to form four ordinary words.

HURCS

USSEO

DERAAP

DUELEX

THE DAILY BLAB

No more scoops

I'm at a loss for words

WHEN THE NEWSPAPER CLOSED, THE WORKERS WERE———

Now arrange the circled letters to form the surprise answer, as suggested by the above cartoon.

Print answer here " ◯◯ - ◯◯◯◯◯◯◯◯ "

JUMBLE®

Unscramble these four Jumbles, one letter to each square, to form four ordinary words.

FIDUL

VERAG

SHUPTY

HIRTHE

That will help me change my image

WHY THE SULTRY SINGER GOT THE BUSINESS OUTFIT.

Now arrange the circled letters to form the surprise answer, as suggested by the above cartoon.

Print answer IT *here* "☐☐☐☐☐☐☐" ☐☐☐

JUMBLE®

Unscramble these four Jumbles, one letter to
each square, to form four ordinary words.

DARAM

GIBLE

LEGBIT

ENVEAL

Not a
chance.
He was
much
better

She was the
clear winner

WHEN THE CANDI-
DATES DISCUSSED
THE ISSUES, THEIR
VIEWS WERE----

Now arrange the circled letters to form the
surprise answer, as suggested by the above
cartoon.

*Print answer
here* " ⬡⬡⬡⬡⬡⬡⬡⬡⬡⬡ "

JUMBLE®

Unscramble these four Jumbles, one letter to
each square, to form four ordinary words.

MYTHE

DAMEF

RESCIB

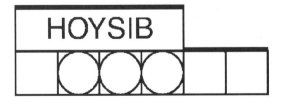

HOYSIB

I remember when I couldn't
run around the block

WHAT HE IMPROVED
WHEN HE JOGGED.

Now arrange the circled letters to form the
surprise answer, as suggested by the above
cartoon.

Print answer here

JUMBLE®

Unscramble these four Jumbles, one letter to each square, to form four ordinary words.

CLOAV

CARPH

DAMALY

GROITE

This is a job for a professional

WHEN THE DO-IT-
YOURSELFER SUM-
MONED A PLUMBER,
HE MADE---

Now arrange the circled letters to form the surprise answer, as suggested by the above cartoon.

Print answer here THE  "  "

JUMBLE®

Unscramble these four Jumbles, one letter to each square, to form four ordinary words.

YONJE

YORIN

BOULED

SHAUTI

Thirty minutes late

So what else is new?

WHAT THE COM-
MUTERS DID WHEN
THE TRAIN FINALLY
ARRIVED.

Now arrange the circled letters to form the surprise answer, as suggested by the above cartoon.

Print answer here

"   "

JUMBLE®

Unscramble these four Jumbles, one letter to
each square, to form four ordinary words.

KELUF

KISLY

RAWLEY

CAJEKT

HOW SHE FELT
AFTER THE
FENDER BENDER.

Now arrange the circled letters to form the
surprise answer, as suggested by the above
cartoon.

Print answer here ◯◯◯◯ A " ◯◯◯◯◯ "

JUMBLE®

Unscramble these four Jumbles, one letter to
each square, to form four ordinary words.

AVVLE

ENZOO

FALACI

ENGALC

Hey, you said
$500. This is
$400

That was
yesterday

WHAT THE SHEP-
HERD GOT WHEN
HE TOOK HIS HERD
TO MARKET.

Now arrange the circled letters to form the
surprise answer, as suggested by the above
cartoon.

*Print answer
here* A "◯◯◯◯◯◯◯◯"

JUMBLE®

Unscramble these four Jumbles, one letter to each square, to form four ordinary words.

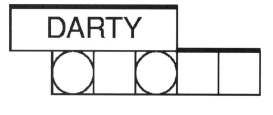

DARTY

PIRRO

MURBEN

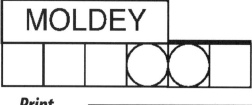

MOLDEY

After you   No, after you

WHAT THE TAILORS FINALLY DID WHEN THEY BOTH NEEDED TO PRESS PANTS.

Now arrange the circled letters to form the surprise answer, as suggested by the above cartoon.

Print answer here

 " ◯◯◯◯◯◯ " IT  ◯◯◯

JUMBLE®

Unscramble these four Jumbles, one letter to
each square, to form four ordinary words.

BARIB

LAASI

SORRAY

PHONYT

I remember
in '49...

That was a
tough year

WELCOME
BACK

THEY ENJOY DIS-
CUSSING OLD TIMES
AT A REUNION.

Now arrange the circled letters to form the
surprise answer, as suggested by the above
cartoon.

*Print
answer
here*

JUMBLE®

Unscramble these four Jumbles, one letter to each square, to form four ordinary words.

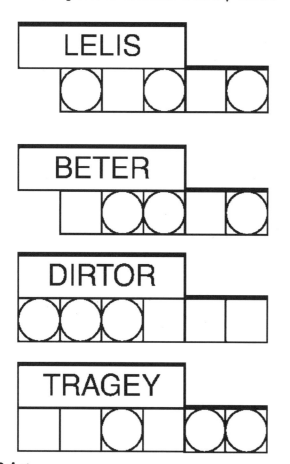

LELIS

BETER

DIRTOR

TRAGEY

Hey, Arnie, what's CPTAH?

Oh, that's easy

THE POSTAL CLERK WAS GOOD AT SOLVING ANAGRAMS BECAUSE HE WAS A——

Now arrange the circled letters to form the surprise answer, as suggested by the above cartoon.

Print answer here

JUMBLE®

Unscramble these four Jumbles, one letter to each square, to form four ordinary words.

RAYRA

MIILT

PUNCOO

UNBOCE

It's yellowing. Just needs water and feeding

WHEN THE GAR-DENER SPOTTED THE DYING SHRUB, HE GOT TO THE----

Now arrange the circled letters to form the surprise answer, as suggested by the above cartoon.

Print answer here " ⬡⬡⬡⬡ " OF THE ⬡⬡⬡⬡⬡⬡⬡

JUMBLE®

Unscramble these four Jumbles, one letter to each square, to form four ordinary words.

PUROG

RYPEK

QUILID

HEHRST

WHEN THE TIPSY
SAILOR WAS SAVED
FROM FALLING
OVERBOARD,
HE WAS---

Now arrange the circled letters to form the surprise answer, as suggested by the above cartoon.

Print answer here ⟨ ◯◯◯◯ ⟩ AND ⟨ ◯◯◯ ⟩

JUMBLE®

Unscramble these four Jumbles, one letter to each square, to form four ordinary words.

JYTET

CNATH

TAYRRM

LETEBE

Soup, pot roast and fresh baked bread

Much better than going out

ENJOYED BY LOVE-BIRDS ON VALENTINE'S DAY.

Now arrange the circled letters to form the surprise answer, as suggested by the above cartoon.

Print answer here A " ⎯⎯⎯⎯⎯⎯ " ⎯⎯⎯⎯

JUMBLE®

Unscramble these four Jumbles, one letter to each square, to form four ordinary words.

CHUVO

RUTTE

SUREDS

STOLJE

You're scalping me

It'll grow back

THE ARMY BARBER TOOK THIS TO SAVE TIME.

Now arrange the circled letters to form the surprise answer, as suggested by the above cartoon.

Print answer here

JUMBLE®

Unscramble these four Jumbles, one letter to
each square, to form four ordinary words.

KERCE

TULIQ

TEPROY

UMSCAP

20 stories of work,
Homer. We'll make
a fortune

WHEN THE LOCK-
SMITH GOT THE
HIGH-RISE JOB,
THE BUILDER
BECAME HIS----

Now arrange the circled letters to form the
surprise answer, as suggested by the above
cartoon.

Print
answer
here "⬡⬡⬡" ⬡⬡⬡⬡⬡⬡⬡⬡

JUMBLE®

Unscramble these four Jumbles, one letter to each square, to form four ordinary words.

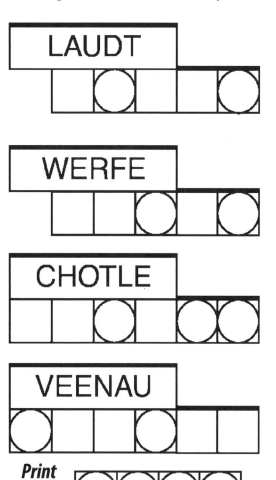

LAUDT

WERFE

CHOTLE

VEENAU

...and he's just a regular guy

Back from the moon

What a feat

THEY LAUDED THE ASTRONAUT BECAUSE HE WAS----

Now arrange the circled letters to form the surprise answer, as suggested by the above cartoon.

Print answer here _____ TO " _____ "

22

JUMBLE®

Unscramble these four Jumbles, one letter to each square, to form four ordinary words.

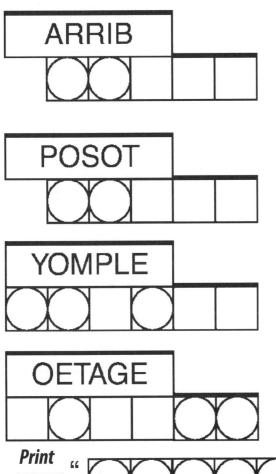

ARRIB

POSOT

YOMPLE

OETAGE

This is very complicated

WHEN THE PIANIST PLAYED THE NEW PIECE, HE FOUND IT WAS----

Now arrange the circled letters to form the surprise answer, as suggested by the above cartoon.

Print answer here " ◯◯◯◯◯◯ - ◯◯◯◯ "

JUMBLE®

Unscramble these four Jumbles, one letter to each square, to form four ordinary words.

TELUF

WILLT

FEYGIF

ZALBER

See how much I lost?

You look the same to me

Yeah, more like 10 pounds

HIS CLAIM OF LOSING 100 POUNDS TURNED OUT TO BE----

Now arrange the circled letters to form the surprise answer, as suggested by the above cartoon.

Print answer here A ⬭⬭⬭ " ⬭⬭⬭ " ⬭⬭⬭

JUMBLE®

Unscramble these four Jumbles, one letter to
each square, to form four ordinary words.

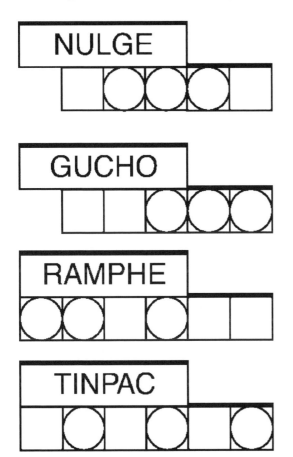

NULGE

GUCHO

RAMPHE

TINPAC

THE TEEN LEFT HIS
CLOTHES ON THE
FLOOR BECAUSE
HE HAD A---

Now arrange the circled letters to form the
surprise answer, as suggested by the above
cartoon.

*Print
answer
here*

JUMBLE®

Unscramble these four Jumbles, one letter to
each square, to form four ordinary words.

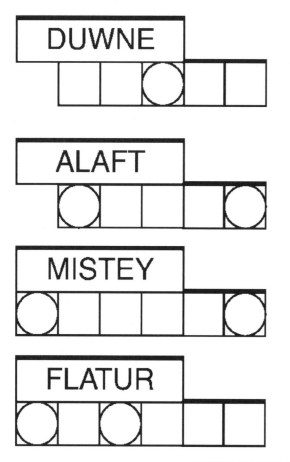

DUWNE

ALAFT

MISTEY

FLATUR

---t-i-o-u-s

Correct!
You win

4041

WHAT HAPPENED
WHEN SHE SPELLED
THE WORD RIGHT.

Now arrange the circled letters to form the
surprise answer, as suggested by the above
cartoon.

Print answer here SHE ◯◯◯ " ◯◯◯◯ "

JUMBLE Sensation

Daily Puzzles

JUMBLE®

Unscramble these four Jumbles, one letter to each square, to form four ordinary words.

POAYS

LAWTZ

YARPOD

MUNCOL

I give up

WHEN THE BROTH-
ERS' PILLOW FIGHT
ENDED, IT WAS----

Now arrange the circled letters to form the surprise answer, as suggested by the above cartoon.

Print answer here " ◯◯◯◯◯ " AND ◯◯◯◯

JUMBLE®

Unscramble these four Jumbles, one letter to each square, to form four ordinary words.

PUTIL

HACOP

DEPLUH

CLORLS

Keep pedaling, Arthur.
I won't let go

WHAT THE
DIVORCED FATHER
GAVE HIS SON.

Now arrange the circled letters to form the surprise answer, as suggested by the above cartoon.

Print answer here

" "

JUMBLE®

Unscramble these four Jumbles, one letter to each square, to form four ordinary words.

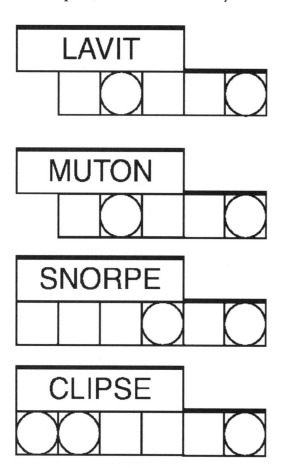

LAVIT

MUTON

SNORPE

CLIPSE

This isn't working

TRYING TO SEW WITH A BROKEN NEEDLE IS----

Now arrange the circled letters to form the surprise answer, as suggested by the above cartoon.

Print answer here " ◯◯◯◯◯◯◯◯◯ "

JUMBLE®

Unscramble these four Jumbles, one letter to
each square, to form four ordinary words.

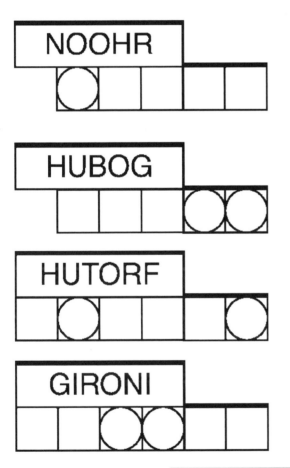

NOOHR

HUBOG

HUTORF

GIRONI

He sold his spread
for millions

HOW THE PIG
FARMER ENDED UP
LIVING WHEN HE
SOLD OUT.

Now arrange the circled letters to form the
surprise answer, as suggested by the above
cartoon.

Print answer here ⬭⬭⬭⬭ ON THE " ⬭⬭⬭ "

JUMBLE

Unscramble these four Jumbles, one letter to
each square, to form four ordinary words.

NENLI

RONOC

STOUBE

JEDAGG

Dangerous
work

He's always
busy

WHAT THE SUC-
CESSFUL DEEP-SEA
DIVER NEVER
WORRIES ABOUT.

Now arrange the circled letters to form the
surprise answer, as suggested by the above
cartoon.

*Print
answer
here*

" "

JUMBLE®

Unscramble these four Jumbles, one letter to
each square, to form four ordinary words.

ELCHE

DOPKE

KALILA

LAWTUN

How 'bout
some
service!

WHAT THE LATE-
ARRIVING GUEST
GAVE THE NIGHT
CLERK.

Now arrange the circled letters to form the
surprise answer, as suggested by the above
cartoon.

**Print
answer A
here**   " ☐☐☐☐☐ - ☐☐ "   ☐☐☐☐☐

JUMBLE®

Unscramble these four Jumbles, one letter to each square, to form four ordinary words.

NOIBS

WALOG

MYLLAC

CINANE

The number is...

She gets great benefits

WHY SHE BECAME
AN OPERATOR.

Now arrange the circled letters to form the surprise answer, as suggested by the above cartoon.

Print answer here IT ◯◯◯ A " ◯◯◯◯◯◯◯ "

JUMBLE®

Unscramble these four Jumbles, one letter to each square, to form four ordinary words.

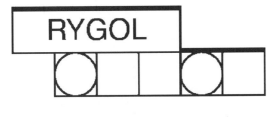

RYGOL

YEEND

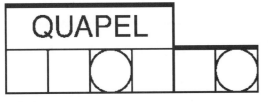

RAMAAD

QUAPEL

Whew! That was tough

It'll be easier going down

WHEN THE CYCLERS COMPLETED THE HILL CLIMB, THEY----

Now arrange the circled letters to form the surprise answer, as suggested by the above cartoon.

Print answer here

 THE " "

JUMBLE®

Unscramble these four Jumbles, one letter to each square, to form four ordinary words.

PEINT

ROPEA

JANGOR

CALDIP

He just signed a big contract

I want to be the best

HE PLAYED SOCCER BECAUSE HE WAS----

Now arrange the circled letters to form the surprise answer, as suggested by the above cartoon.

Print answer here " ◯◯◯◯ " ◯◯◯◯◯◯◯◯◯◯

JUMBLE®

Unscramble these four Jumbles, one letter to each square, to form four ordinary words.

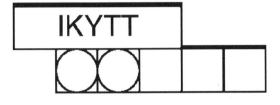

IKYTT

NALUN

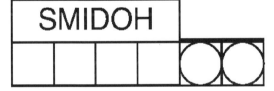

SMIDOH

YINJET

Hilda must have gained 50 pounds

Shh. She's very sensitive

OFTEN GOES ALONG WITH A THICK BODY.

Now arrange the circled letters to form the surprise answer, as suggested by the above cartoon.

Print answer here A

37

JUMBLE®

Unscramble these four Jumbles, one letter to
each square, to form four ordinary words.

CHABT

WILEH

MUTTOS

HELSIG

I baked you a
chocolate cake

I made
some
cookies

WHAT THE HOSTESS
SAID WHEN HER
GUESTS BROUGHT
DESSERT.

Now arrange the circled letters to form the
surprise answer, as suggested by the above
cartoon.

Print
answer
here
 ' □ SO "  "

JUMBLE®

Unscramble these four Jumbles, one letter to
each square, to form four ordinary words.

AFMEL

RADIC

HATTOR

TESKAB

You do the
dishes

What about
her?

Not
me

GIVING KIDS HOUSE-
HOLD DUTIES CAN
BE A---

Now arrange the circled letters to form the
surprise answer, as suggested by the above
cartoon.

*Print
answer
here*

IN

JUMBLE®

Unscramble these four Jumbles, one letter to each square, to form four ordinary words.

EVING

ALYMN

DEBLOH

RODIAH

I'll get that for you

WHAT THE LITTLE OLD CLOCKMAKER'S HELPER DID.

Now arrange the circled letters to form the surprise answer, as suggested by the above cartoon.

Print answer here

A " "

JUMBLE®

Unscramble these four Jumbles, one letter to
each square, to form four ordinary words.

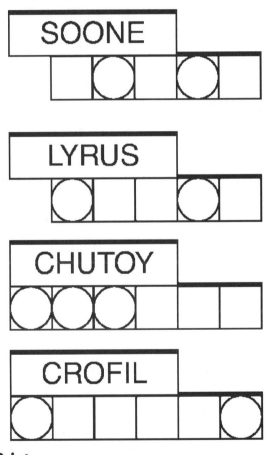

SOONE

LYRUS

CHUTOY

CROFIL

Safe!

You missed the big play

I was getting a crowd shot

WHY THE SPORTS
CAMERAMAN WAS
FIRED.

Now arrange the circled letters to form the
surprise answer, as suggested by the above
cartoon.

*Print
answer
here*   HE  HIS "  "

JUMBLE®

Unscramble these four Jumbles, one letter to
each square, to form four ordinary words.

TYTUN

ROALF

SOUXED

TOSEFF

Quite a
collection
you've got
here

USUALLY FOUND AT
A TAXIDERMY SHOP.

Now arrange the circled letters to form the
surprise answer, as suggested by the above
cartoon.

Print
answer
here

 OF "  "

42

JUMBLE®

Unscramble these four Jumbles, one letter to each square, to form four ordinary words.

ALCKO

BLEEL

UPDELD

UNTAGO

It just fell

But don't worry, we'll fix it

WHAT THE TWINS GAVE MOM WHEN THE LAMP FELL.

Now arrange the circled letters to form the surprise answer, as suggested by the above cartoon.

Print answer here " ◯◯◯◯◯◯ " ◯◯◯◯

JUMBLE®

Unscramble these four Jumbles, one letter to
each square, to form four ordinary words.

RIFAR

OPYPP

SMABAL

EMBURP

My new high heels
will be ruined

SOUND RIGHT, BUT
VERY WRONG, TO
CROSS A FLOODED
STREET.

Now arrange the circled letters to form the
surprise answer, as suggested by the above
cartoon.

*Print
answer
here* A ◯◯◯◯ OF " ◯◯◯◯◯ "

JUMBLE®

Unscramble these four Jumbles, one letter to each square, to form four ordinary words.

ARSYC

MILOB

WOBELL

GREDLE

Where have you been?

Have you been drinking?

WHAT HAPPENED
WHEN HE CAME
HOME STEWED?

Now arrange the circled letters to form the surprise answer, as suggested by the above cartoon.

 **Print answer here** HE ◯◯◯ " ◯◯◯◯◯◯◯◯ "

JUMBLE®

Unscramble these four Jumbles, one letter to
each square, to form four ordinary words.

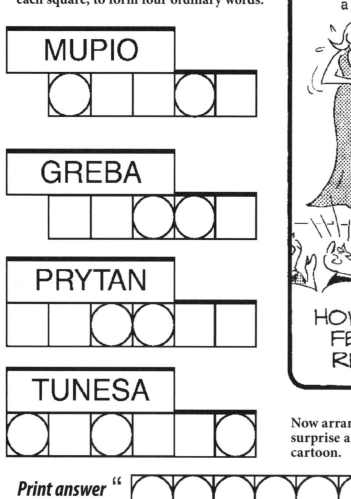

MUPIO

GREBA

PRYTAN

TUNESA

I feel like
a limp rag

She
practiced
for
weeks

HOW THE HARPIST
FELT WHEN THE
RECITAL ENDED.

Now arrange the circled letters to form the
surprise answer, as suggested by the above
cartoon.

*Print answer
here* " ⬚⬚⬚⬚⬚⬚ " ⬚⬚⬚

JUMBLE®

Unscramble these four Jumbles, one letter to each square, to form four ordinary words.

ROHAB

PRAVO

CANOBE

GEEREM

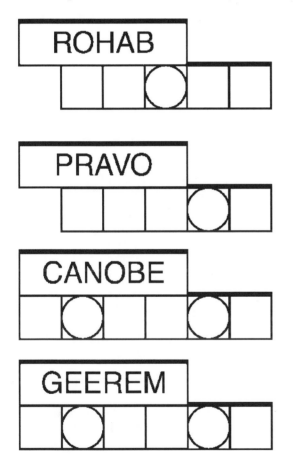

Do you play bridge?

How about dominos?

Games are for children

WHAT THE HOSTS WISHED THEIR GUESTS WOULD DO.

Now arrange the circled letters to form the surprise answer, as suggested by the above cartoon.

Print answer here

JUMBLE®

Unscramble these four Jumbles, one letter to each square, to form four ordinary words.

EGGOR

INHEW

BOIFLE

BARTIL

It's your turn to make the coffee

No, it's yours

WHEN THE SERVERS DIDN'T GET ALONG, THERE WAS A---

Now arrange the circled letters to form the surprise answer, as suggested by the above cartoon.

Print answer here

JUMBLE®

Unscramble these four Jumbles, one letter to each square, to form four ordinary words.

MIRPE

GUNTS

LATBEL

SAFTIE

He's catching his breath and forty winks

FINISH LINE

HOW THE COACH DESCRIBED THE TIRED SPRINTER.

Now arrange the circled letters to form the surprise answer, as suggested by the above cartoon.

Print answer here

◯◯◯◯ , ◯◯◯◯◯◯◯

JUMBLE®

Unscramble these four Jumbles, one letter to each square, to form four ordinary words.

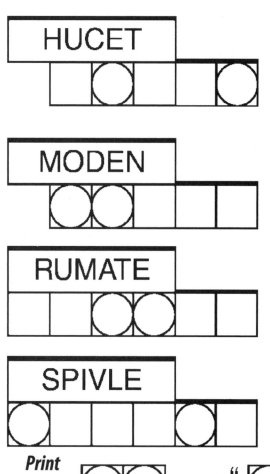

HUCET

MODEN

RUMATE

SPIVLE

Let it ring.
Concentrate.

WHY THE YOGA
INSTRUCTOR DIDN'T
ANSWER THE PHONE.

Now arrange the circled letters to form the surprise answer, as suggested by the above cartoon.

Print answer here ⎯ WAS " ⎯ "

JUMBLE®

Unscramble these four Jumbles, one letter to each square, to form four ordinary words.

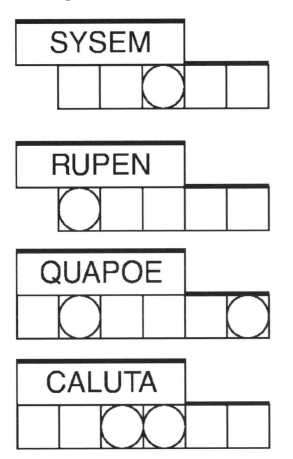

SYSEM

RUPEN

QUAPOE

CALUTA

You should've finished the stairs by now

Taking a break, Boss

WHAT THE FORE-MAN WANTED THE LAZY CARPENTER TO DO.

Now arrange the circled letters to form the surprise answer, as suggested by the above cartoon.

Print answer here " ⃝⃝⃝⃝ " IT ⃝⃝

JUMBLE®

Unscramble these four Jumbles, one letter to
each square, to form four ordinary words.

ROCCU

WORBE

LAFTOA

CUDLAN

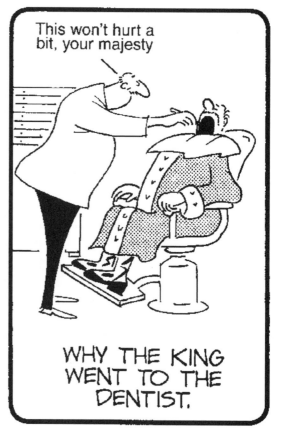

This won't hurt a
bit, your majesty

WHY THE KING
WENT TO THE
DENTIST.

Now arrange the circled letters to form the
surprise answer, as suggested by the above
cartoon.

*Print answer
here*

⬜⬜⬜ A " ⬜⬜⬜⬜⬜ "

JUMBLE®

Unscramble these four Jumbles, one letter to each square, to form four ordinary words.

ITTYD

ODARR

BROIMD

HARANG

You call this short?

I'm not paying

I didn't ask for frizzy

WHAT THE UNHAPPY CUSTOMERS GAVE THE BEAUTY SHOP OWNER.

Now arrange the circled letters to form the surprise answer, as suggested by the above cartoon.

Print answer A
here

JUMBLE®

Unscramble these four Jumbles, one letter to
each square, to form four ordinary words.

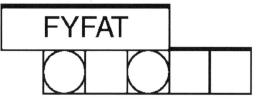

FYFAT

MANUH

PRONAD

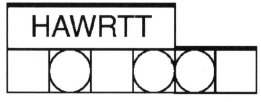

HAWRTT

All the
way
to the
bottom?

DEEP SEA DIVING
CAN BE THIS.

Now arrange the circled letters to form the
surprise answer, as suggested by the above
cartoon.

**Print
answer
here**

TO " "

JUMBLE®

Unscramble these four Jumbles, one letter to
each square, to form four ordinary words.

DITIO

DEWEG

ANNAAB

HAWLIE

It's time to
think about
retiring

WHAT THE WATCH-
MAKER DECIDED
TO DO AS HE GOT
ON IN YEARS.

Now arrange the circled letters to form the
surprise answer, as suggested by the above
cartoon.

Print answer here "  "

JUMBLE®

Unscramble these four Jumbles, one letter to each square, to form four ordinary words.

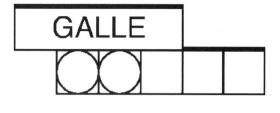

GALLE

GUZAE

GINPYT

RACLIG

When you're finished you can slice and dice them

Hey, this is fun

HE HELPED HIS WIFE CLEAN THE VEGETABLES AND FOUND THE TASK——

Now arrange the circled letters to form the surprise answer, as suggested by the above cartoon.

Print answer here ◯ - ◯◯◯◯◯◯◯

JUMBLE®

Unscramble these four Jumbles, one letter to
each square, to form four ordinary words.

SOURE

NALAC

TUILED

FLOUWE

Done! No
more cavity!

You're the
best, Doc

WHAT A SUCCESSFUL
DENTIST DOES.

Now arrange the circled letters to form the
surprise answer, as suggested by the above
cartoon.

*Print
answer
here* " ⬡⬡⬡⬡⬡⬡ " A ⬡⬡⬡⬡

JUMBLE®

Unscramble these four Jumbles, one letter to each square, to form four ordinary words.

NURSP

KRIHE

TINKTE

INQUAT

Don't forget. Home by ten

I'm not a baby, you know

THE FIRST THING A TEENAGER WILL DO.

Now arrange the circled letters to form the surprise answer, as suggested by the above cartoon.

Print answer here

JUMBLE®

Unscramble these four Jumbles, one letter to
each square, to form four ordinary words.

BOUMG

PRAAT

HORKES

CADETH

Forty bucks. Take
it or leave it

WHAT THE UMBRELLA
SALESMAN DID
DURING THE RAIN-
STORM.

Now arrange the circled letters to form the
surprise answer, as suggested by the above
cartoon.

*Print
answer
here*

HE " ⬡⬡⬡⬡⬡⬡ " ⬡⬡⬡⬡

JUMBLE®

Unscramble these four Jumbles, one letter to
each square, to form four ordinary words.

TACUE

EVIRT

INOUSC

INCLOU

Get out of
my house!

WHEN HE DID A
POOR JOB
INSTALLING THE
WINDOW TREAT-
MENT, IT WAS----

Now arrange the circled letters to form the
surprise answer, as suggested by the above
cartoon.

Print answer here "⬡⬡⬡⬡⬡⬡⬡⬡"

60

JUMBLE®

Unscramble these four Jumbles, one letter to
each square, to form four ordinary words.

PRUTE

KICHT

DAILNG

YURTIP

#$%&*!!
It slipped!

Dry
your
hand

WHAT THE BOWLER
USED WHEN HIS
BALL WENT ASTRAY.

Now arrange the circled letters to form the
surprise answer, as suggested by the above
cartoon.

Print
answer
here

"⬭⬭⬭⬭⬭⬭⬭" ⬭⬭⬭⬭

JUMBLE®

Unscramble these four Jumbles, one letter to
each square, to form four ordinary words.

UNDAT

TESED

THINEW

GLOUEY

That's enough for today,
Charlie. I'm going to
the races

But this
will spoil

WHY THE BAKER
DIDN'T MAKE MUCH
MONEY.

Now arrange the circled letters to form the
surprise answer, as suggested by the above
cartoon.

**Print
answer
here**   HE 〇〇〇〇〇〇 HIS " 〇〇〇〇〇 "

JUMBLE®

Unscramble these four Jumbles, one letter to
each square, to form four ordinary words.

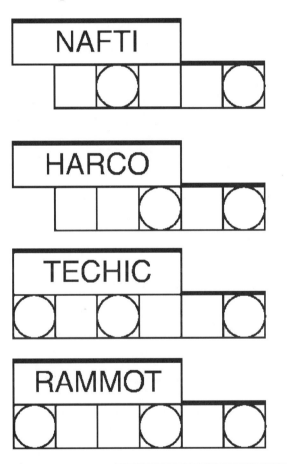

NAFTI

HARCO

TECHIC

RAMMOT

How 'bout dinner?

A perfect couple

WHEN THEY MET
ON THE TENNIS
COURT AND LATER
MARRIED, IT WAS
A- - - -

Now arrange the circled letters to form the
surprise answer, as suggested by the above
cartoon.

Print answer
here

JUMBLE®

Unscramble these four Jumbles, one letter to
each square, to form four ordinary words.

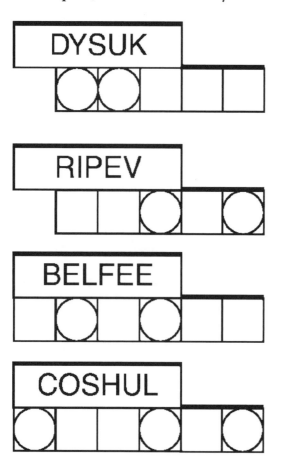

DYSUK

RIPEV

BELFEE

COSHUL

First the
eyebrows, then
the eyelashes

WHAT THE BEAUTI-
CIANS DID BEFORE
THE COSMETICS
EXAM.

Now arrange the circled letters to form the
surprise answer, as suggested by the above
cartoon.

*Print answer
here* "   "

64

JUMBLE®

Unscramble these four Jumbles, one letter to each square, to form four ordinary words.

RUSIV

GEISE

RAWSEN

SCAFIO

EASILY RAISED AT MORNING ROLL CALL.

Now arrange the circled letters to form the surprise answer, as suggested by the above cartoon.

Print answer here

 ,

JUMBLE®

Unscramble these four Jumbles, one letter to each square, to form four ordinary words.

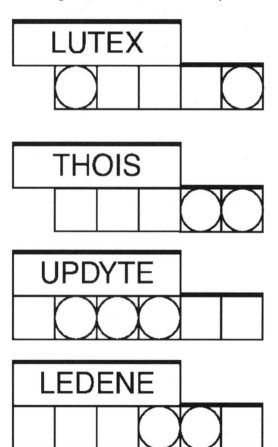

LUTEX

THOIS

UPDYTE

LEDENE

One for
the road

Your bill,
sir

WHAT THE HOTEL
GUEST DID BEFORE
HE SETTLED DOWN
FOR THE NIGHT.

Now arrange the circled letters to form the
surprise answer, as suggested by the above
cartoon.

Print answer here

JUMBLE®

Unscramble these four Jumbles, one letter to each square, to form four ordinary words.

NACYF

TYRID

TICEOP

POYNAC

I obeyed all the rules of the road

You did well

PASSING HIS DRI-VER'S TEST WAS---

Now arrange the circled letters to form the surprise answer, as suggested by the above cartoon.

Print answer here

JUMBLE®

Unscramble these four Jumbles, one letter to
each square, to form four ordinary words.

WARBL

YAHNE

DROPEN

LOBIED

Strong as
an ox

He's hard
to tackle

WHAT THE FARM-
BOY DID ON THE
FOOTBALL FIELD.

Now arrange the circled letters to form the
surprise answer, as suggested by the above
cartoon.

Print
answer
here

" "

JUMBLE®

Unscramble these four Jumbles, one letter to each square, to form four ordinary words.

TIFUR

MILPE

MIGNIT

CAYGEN

That's my string

We're all tangled up

WHEN THE SCOUTS HAD A KNOT-MAKING CONTEST, IT TURNED INTO A----

Now arrange the circled letters to form the surprise answer, as suggested by the above cartoon.

Print answer here " ◯◯◯ " ◯◯◯◯

JUMBLE®

Unscramble these four Jumbles, one letter to each square, to form four ordinary words.

WAHSS

LAINF

VETOMI

REFLOG

Let's follow this opening in the ice

WHAT THE SCIENTISTS DECIDED TO DO WHEN THEY STUDIED THE ICEBERGS.

Now arrange the circled letters to form the surprise answer, as suggested by the above cartoon.

Print answer here   □□ □□□□ THE " □□□□ "

70

JUMBLE®

Unscramble these four Jumbles, one letter to
each square, to form four ordinary words.

MUTOH

NIORB

PRAMTE

REDUME

Extra homework
for everyone

WHEN THE CLASS
GOT ROWDY, THE
MATH TEACHER DID
A----

Now arrange the circled letters to form the
surprise answer, as suggested by the above
cartoon.

*Print
answer
here* " ⬭⬭⬭⬭⬭⬭ " ON ⬭⬭⬭⬭

JUMBLE®

Unscramble these four Jumbles, one letter to each square, to form four ordinary words.

LELOH

DOLDY

LENPOL

GAAMED

He's faster than lightning

WHAT THE GREY-HOUND TURNED INTO WHEN HE RACED AROUND THE TRACK.

Now arrange the circled letters to form the surprise answer, as suggested by the above cartoon.

Print answer here A " ☐☐☐ " ☐☐☐

JUMBLE®

Unscramble these four Jumbles, one letter to
each square, to form four ordinary words.

GAREW

FECOR

HAVEEB

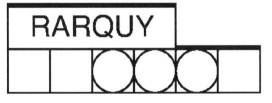

RARQUY

It makes a good
doorstop

WHEN HE GOT A
DEAD BATTERY
FROM THE JUNK-
YARD, IT WAS----

Now arrange the circled letters to form the
surprise answer, as suggested by the above
cartoon.

*Print
answer
here*

 OF "  "

JUMBLE®

Unscramble these four Jumbles, one letter to
each square, to form four ordinary words.

HOYNE

ADECK

RYLAIF

YARPIC

Come in. May I offer
you a liqueur?

A NICE WELCOME.

Now arrange the circled letters to form the
surprise answer, as suggested by the above
cartoon.

Print answer here " ⬡⬡⬡⬡⬡⬡⬡ "

JUMBLE®

Unscramble these four Jumbles, one letter to each square, to form four ordinary words.

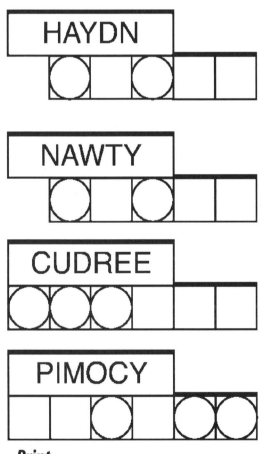

HAYDN

NAWTY

CUDREE

PIMOCY

Hey! It's Joey the Nose

Hi, boys

WHEN THE GANG-STER WENT TO PRISON HE BECAME PART OF---

Now arrange the circled letters to form the surprise answer, as suggested by the above cartoon.

Print answer here

☐☐☐ " ☐☐ " ☐☐☐☐☐☐

JUMBLE®

Unscramble these four Jumbles, one letter to each square, to form four ordinary words.

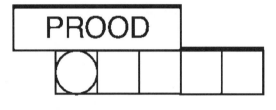

PROOD

LALIV

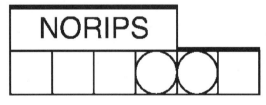

PEMEXT

NORIPS

Sorry, I tripped

THIS CAN HAPPEN TO "MODELS,"

Now arrange the circled letters to form the surprise answer, as suggested by the above cartoon.

Print answer here "  "

JUMBLE®

Unscramble these four Jumbles, one letter to each square, to form four ordinary words.

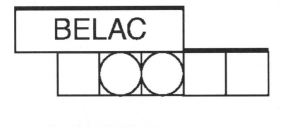

BELAC

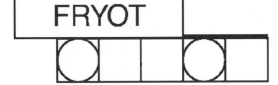

FRYOT

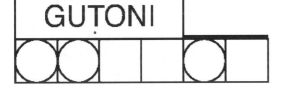

GUTONI

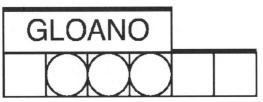

GLOANO

I love it. I feel like a new person

WHAT SHE GOT FROM HER NEW HAIR STYLE.

Now arrange the circled letters to form the surprise answer, as suggested by the above cartoon.

Print answer here

IT

JUMBLE®

Unscramble these four Jumbles, one letter to
each square, to form four ordinary words.

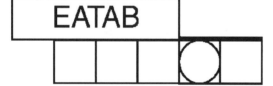

UGLIE

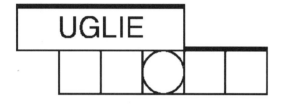

EATAB

QUIETY

TOFFES

I'm not paying.
that looks
awful

WHEN THE YOUNG
LAD TRIED ON THE
TAILORED SUIT,
MOM HAD A ---

Now arrange the circled letters to form the
surprise answer, as suggested by the above
cartoon.

Print answer here

JUMBLE®

Unscramble these four Jumbles, one letter to
each square, to form four ordinary words.

ZELAH

YOSUL

EXDULP

COIBED

It's so nice
of you to say

She's not as
nice as she seems

NOT A GOOD WAY
TO PICK A FRIEND.

Now arrange the circled letters to form the
surprise answer, as suggested by the above
cartoon.

Print answer here TO ☐☐☐☐☐☐

JUMBLE®

Unscramble these four Jumbles, one letter to
each square, to form four ordinary words.

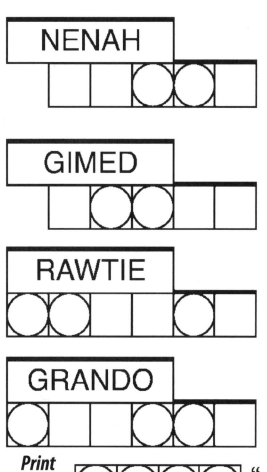

NENAH

GIMED

RAWTIE

GRANDO

I've been waiting
for an hour.
GOODBYE

WHEN HE WAS LATE
FOR THEIR BEACH
DATE, SHE WAS ---

Now arrange the circled letters to form the
surprise answer, as suggested by the above
cartoon.

*Print
answer
here*

" "

JUMBLE®

Unscramble these four Jumbles, one letter to each square, to form four ordinary words.

TAXEC

THECK

KROMES

PERRAY

It keeps falling apart

WHAT THE FARMER EXPERIENCED WHEN HE BEGAN BUILDING A STONE WALL.

Now arrange the circled letters to form the surprise answer, as suggested by the above cartoon.

Print answer here A " ◯◯◯◯◯ " ◯◯◯◯◯◯

JUMBLE®

Unscramble these four Jumbles, one letter to each square, to form four ordinary words.

LUBLY

FIGER

DORINO

YARWIA

I can't concentrate

GO TEAM

WHEN THE PROBLEM WAS DIFFICULT TO SOLVE, THE STUDENT SAVED IT FOR A ---

Now arrange the circled letters to form the surprise answer, as suggested by the above cartoon.

Print answer here " ⬡⬡⬡⬡⬡⬡ " ⬡⬡⬡

JUMBLE®

Unscramble these four Jumbles, one letter to
each square, to form four ordinary words.

REIND

TOAPI

NOSPER

CUPSAM

How much?

$25.00

Flowers by Flo

SHARED BY A
FLOWER STEM AND A
FLORIST SHOP.

Now arrange the circled letters to form the
surprise answer, as suggested by the above
cartoon.

***Print
answer
here***   ◯◯◯◯◯ OF ◯◯◯◯◯◯◯

JUMBLE®

Unscramble these four Jumbles, one letter to each square, to form four ordinary words.

KESTO

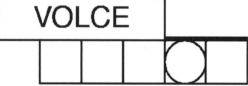

VOLCE

DIMADY

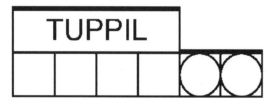

TUPPIL

Drinks for everyone

Hey!
It's Wally

WHEN HE RETURNED
TO THE OLD
HANGOUT,
HE PAID ---

Now arrange the circled letters to form the surprise answer, as suggested by the above cartoon.

Print answer here A

JUMBLE®

Unscramble these four Jumbles, one letter to
each square, to form four ordinary words.

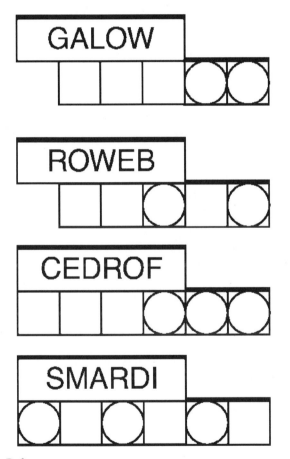

GALOW

ROWEB

CEDROF

SMARDI

WHAT THE ARTIST
AND THE SMASH
HIT MUSICAL
HAD IN COMMON,

Now arrange the circled letters to form the
surprise answer, as suggested by the above
cartoon.

**Print
answer** THEY
here

JUMBLE®

Unscramble these four Jumbles, one letter to each square, to form four ordinary words.

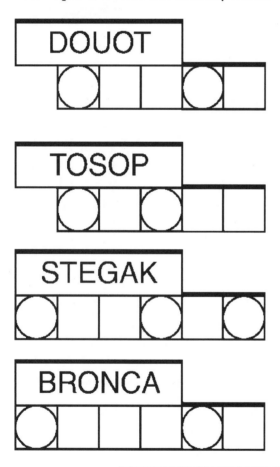

DOUOT

TOSOP

STEGAK

BRONCA

His family is loaded with blue chip shares

HER FIANCÉ WAS QUITE A CATCH BECAUSE HE CAME FROM ----

Now arrange the circled letters to form the surprise answer, as suggested by the above cartoon.

Print answer here

 "  "

JUMBLE®

Unscramble these four Jumbles, one letter to each square, to form four ordinary words.

YAARR

MYHRE

FELICK

DUQILI

So the interest is 7.25

4.57%
5.25%
7.25%
8.00%
9.25%
9.99%

USED BY A BANKER TO MAKE A POINT.

Now arrange the circled letters to form the surprise answer, as suggested by the above cartoon.

Print answer here A ☐☐☐☐☐☐☐

JUMBLE®

Unscramble these four Jumbles, one letter to
each square, to form four ordinary words.

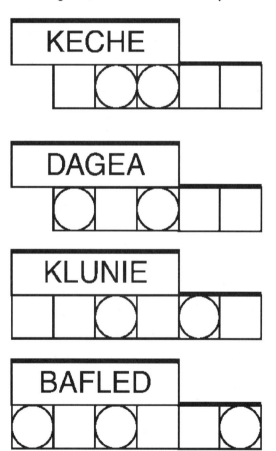

KECHE

DAGEA

KLUNIE

BAFLED

Needs work

WHEN THE BAKER
HAD AN IDEA FOR A
NEW CAKE, IT TURNED
OUT TO BE---

Now arrange the circled letters to form the
surprise answer, as suggested by the above
cartoon.

Print answer here

88

JUMBLE®

Unscramble these four Jumbles, one letter to
each square, to form four ordinary words.

DUGAR

RABEG

REVORF

LOCHOS

Sweet dreams

Night, Daddy

WHAT THE INSURANCE
AGENT'S DAUGHTER
GOT WHEN HE
TUCKED HER IN,

Now arrange the circled letters to form the
surprise answer, as suggested by the above
cartoon.

*Print
answer
here*

JUMBLE®

Unscramble these four Jumbles, one letter to
each square, to form four ordinary words.

MOFUR

COUPH

DORRAM

APTECK

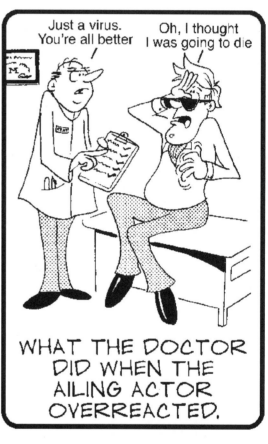

WHAT THE DOCTOR
DID WHEN THE
AILING ACTOR
OVERREACTED.

Now arrange the circled letters to form the
surprise answer, as suggested by the above
cartoon.

*Print answer
here*

THE " "

PUZZLE
89

JUMBLE®

Unscramble these four Jumbles, one letter to
each square, to form four ordinary words.

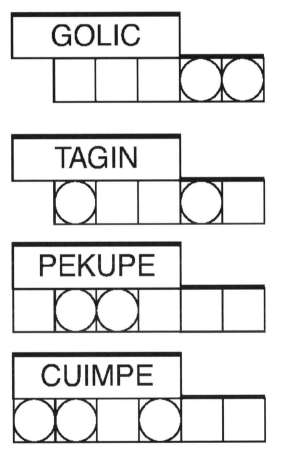

GOLIC

TAGIN

PEKUPE

CUIMPE

The same
steady work

How's things?

WITH THE ECONOMY
DOWN, THE GARBAGE
COLLECTOR SAID
BUSINESS WAS ---

Now arrange the circled letters to form the
surprise answer, as suggested by the above
cartoon.

Print answer here

JUMBLE®

Unscramble these four Jumbles, one letter to
each square, to form four ordinary words.

MUGAT

ELLAD

FRIVED

RAYPOD

What do you think about doing that?

WHEN HER HUSBAND
WANTED TO TAKE A
HOT-AIR BALLOON
RIDE, HE ----

Now arrange the circled letters to form the
surprise answer, as suggested by the above
cartoon.

**Print
answer
here** " ⬡⬡⬡⬡⬡⬡⬡ " THE ⬡⬡⬡⬡

JUMBLE.

Unscramble these four Jumbles, one letter to each square, to form four ordinary words.

WEDIP

NOVEM

ROFTIP

TANIED

I want to cover sports

He's our star pitcher

GO TIGERS

"LEFTY" JOINED THE SCHOOL NEWSPAPER BECAUSE HE WAS ----

Now arrange the circled letters to form the surprise answer, as suggested by the above cartoon.

Print answer here " ⬡⬡⬡⬡⬡ " ⬡⬡⬡⬡⬡⬡

JUMBLE®

Unscramble these four Jumbles, one letter to
each square, to form four ordinary words.

DALGE

YASID

SOLJET

YUPERN

I still have to
do the dishes
and the floors

THE TEEN DID THE
WASH BECAUSE IT
WAS PART
OF HER – – –

Now arrange the circled letters to form the
surprise answer, as suggested by the above
cartoon.

*Print
answer
here*

"⃝⃝⃝⃝⃝⃝⃝" ⃝⃝⃝⃝

JUMBLE®

Unscramble these four Jumbles, one letter to
each square, to form four ordinary words.

AVERB

SUGES

VISPLE

RUSTEY

WHAT THE BOXERS
EXCHANGED BEFORE
THE BIG FIGHT.

Now arrange the circled letters to form the
surprise answer, as suggested by the above
cartoon.

**Print
answer
here**

95

JUMBLE®

Unscramble these four Jumbles, one letter to
each square, to form four ordinary words.

TUSEA

RICHA

QUEETA

VODURE

WHEN THE GENERAL
WENT TO BED, HIS
PILLOW BECAME
HIS – – –

Now arrange the circled letters to form the
surprise answer, as suggested by the above
cartoon.

*Print
answer
here*   "   "

JUMBLE®

Unscramble these four Jumbles, one letter to
each square, to form four ordinary words.

HAWTE

PREKO

TRUFOH

BOYDUL

OUCH!

Run for the
water

WHAT THE BATHERS
DID WHEN THEY HIT
THE BURNING SAND

Now arrange the circled letters to form the
surprise answer, as suggested by the above
cartoon.

*Print
answer
here* "◯◯◯ ◯◯◯◯◯◯" IT

JUMBLE®

Unscramble these four Jumbles, one letter to each square, to form four ordinary words.

NYOME

ERNIL

DARWIN

CINFAG

TODAY A CELL PHONE CAN DO THIS.

Now arrange the circled letters to form the surprise answer, as suggested by the above cartoon.

Print answer here

IN THE

JUMBLE®

Unscramble these four Jumbles, one letter to
each square, to form four ordinary words.

WANTY

VINGY

GULJEG

CALAPE

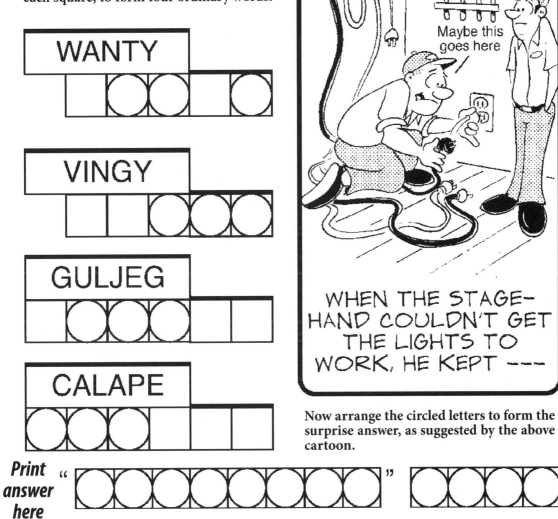

Maybe this
goes here

WHEN THE STAGE-
HAND COULDN'T GET
THE LIGHTS TO
WORK, HE KEPT ----

Now arrange the circled letters to form the
surprise answer, as suggested by the above
cartoon.

**Print
answer
here**

" ⃝⃝⃝⃝⃝⃝⃝⃝ "   ⃝⃝⃝⃝

JUMBLE®

Unscramble these four Jumbles, one letter to each square, to form four ordinary words.

TASID

DIEFT

BLOGON

SAQUEY

He learned the formations in no time

THE TROMBONIST JOINED THE MARCH-ING BAND BECAUSE HE KNEW THE ---

Now arrange the circled letters to form the surprise answer, as suggested by the above cartoon.

Print answer here ⟨◯◯◯⟩ AND ⟨◯◯◯◯◯⟩

JUMBLE

Unscramble these four Jumbles, one letter to
each square, to form four ordinary words.

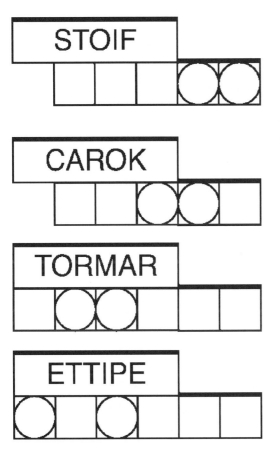

STOIF

CAROK

TORMAR

ETTIPE

You're all red

I fell
asleep

WHAT THE OVER-
WEIGHT SUNBATHER
EXPERIENCED AT
THE BEACH.

Now arrange the circled letters to form the
surprise answer, as suggested by the above
cartoon.

Print answer A "◯◯◯" ◯◯◯◯◯◯
here

JUMBLE®

Unscramble these four Jumbles, one letter to
each square, to form four ordinary words.

URRJO

LECCY

BLUMJE

INFISH

She's been 39
for years

A GOOD WAY TO
KEEP YOUR AGE.

Now arrange the circled letters to form the
surprise answer, as suggested by the above
cartoon.

Print answer here TO

JUMBLE®

Unscramble these four Jumbles, one letter to each square, to form four ordinary words.

BUCCI

TOXEL

VEGASA

UCCSAU

Bye, dear

Gotta run

WHAT HE DID WHEN HE LEFT FOR THE OFFICE.

Now arrange the circled letters to form the surprise answer, as suggested by the above cartoon.

Print answer here ○○○ THE "○○○○"

JUMBLE®

Unscramble these four Jumbles, one letter to
each square, to form four ordinary words.

SPAWM

TREHB

TOAPIE

GALEGH

Are you going
to pay these?

Just add them
to the pile

HOW HE KEPT
THEIR BILLS DOWN.

Now arrange the circled letters to form the
surprise answer, as suggested by the above
cartoon.

*Print
answer
here* A

JUMBLE®

Unscramble these four Jumbles, one letter to each square, to form four ordinary words.

RAWGE

SOITH

KOVINE

WOTOWK

No change   I win the bet

WHAT SHE LOST ON THE 14-DAY DIET.

Now arrange the circled letters to form the surprise answer, as suggested by the above cartoon.

Print answer here ⬡⬡⬡ ⬡⬡⬡⬡⬡

JUMBLE®

Unscramble these four Jumbles, one letter to each square, to form four ordinary words.

MEWNO

REDON

GOHBUT

COASIF

Ouch!

A COMMON WAY TO START OUT WHEN LEARNING TO DANCE.

Now arrange the circled letters to form the surprise answer, as suggested by the above cartoon.

Print answer here ON THE ⬡⬡⬡⬡⬡ ⬡⬡⬡⬡

JUMBLE®

Unscramble these four Jumbles, one letter to each square, to form four ordinary words.

TOIDT

KLACH

ONSOAL

CUMAUV

WHAT HE NEEDED
TO HEAT
HIS HOUSE.

Now arrange the circled letters to form the surprise answer, as suggested by the above cartoon.

Print answer here " ◯◯◯◯ " ◯◯◯◯

JUMBLE®

Unscramble these four Jumbles, one letter to
each square, to form four ordinary words.

PIRGE

HUSBY

CACTEN

MYFAIL

It comes with
a 30,000 mile
tire guarantee **SALE!**

$$$

USUALLY LAST
FOR YEARS
ON NEW CARS.

Now arrange the circled letters to form the
surprise answer, as suggested by the above
cartoon.

Print answer here

JUMBLE®

Unscramble these four Jumbles, one letter to each square, to form four ordinary words.

YUJIC

DEBIP

ANOBBO

JETNUK

Where's the meat?

WHEN THE SALES-MAN ATE AT THE SEA-FOOD RESTAURANT, HE HAD A ---

Now arrange the circled letters to form the surprise answer, as suggested by the above cartoon.

Print answer here ⬡⬡⬡⬡ TO ⬡⬡⬡⬡

JUMBLE®

Unscramble these four Jumbles, one letter to
each square, to form four ordinary words.

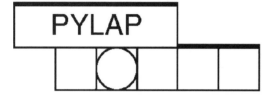

PYLAP

HUTOM

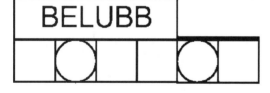

BELUBB

SHMAIF

This should take
care of everything

WHAT THE ACCIDENT
VICTIM GOT FOR
THE BUMP ON
HIS HEAD.

Now arrange the circled letters to form the
surprise answer, as suggested by the above
cartoon.

Print answer here A "  "

110

JUMBLE®

Unscramble these four Jumbles, one letter to each square, to form four ordinary words.

GESIE

FLOTY

PHONIS

MANCEP

Mommy, this doesn't work

AN UNSHARPENED PENCIL IS THIS.

Now arrange the circled letters to form the surprise answer, as suggested by the above cartoon.

Print answer here

JUMBLE®

Unscramble these four Jumbles, one letter to each square, to form four ordinary words.

DURIL

HAIKK

CRADEA

OXENTS

I hear he's having an affair

She just got a promotion

WHAT THE LADIES DID WHEN THEY CLEANED THE OFFICE.

Now arrange the circled letters to form the surprise answer, as suggested by the above cartoon.

Print answer here

 THE "  "

JUMBLE®

Unscramble these four Jumbles, one letter to
each square, to form four ordinary words.

TOLCH

BOVAR

LAWVOA

RUQUOM

It's like this
every year

WHEN THE TIRE
DEALERS HELD THEIR
DANCE, IT TURNED
INTO A ---

Now arrange the circled letters to form the
surprise answer, as suggested by the above
cartoon.

Print answer here " ◯◯◯◯◯◯◯ "

113

JUMBLE®

Unscramble these four Jumbles, one letter to
each square, to form four ordinary words.

HOLEL

CUSTO

ROCCEE

CRUVSY

We're the champs!

HOME 20 AWAY 00

WHAT THE FOOTBALL
TEAM ACHIEVED WHEN
THEY WON 20-0.

Now arrange the circled letters to form the
surprise answer, as suggested by the above
cartoon.

*Print
answer
here* A

JUMBLE®

Unscramble these four Jumbles, one letter to each square, to form four ordinary words.

BORNI

YIRDT

DIBOLE

BRAFIC

Do you disco?

Bell bottoms?

2/14

WHEN HE WORE THE OUTDATED CORDUROYS, HE WAS ---

Now arrange the circled letters to form the surprise answer, as suggested by the above cartoon.

Print answer here "  "

JUMBLE®

Unscramble these four Jumbles, one letter to
each square, to form four ordinary words.

GUFED

CEEJT

URRUMM

CAUVIN

How can you do
that all day?

It's an
honest job

WHAT HE FACED
WHEN HE WORKED AT
THE CEMETERY.

Now arrange the circled letters to form the
surprise answer, as suggested by the above
cartoon.

**Print
answer** A "⬡⬡⬡⬡⬡" ⬡⬡⬡⬡⬡⬡
here

JUMBLE®

Unscramble these four Jumbles, one letter to each square, to form four ordinary words.

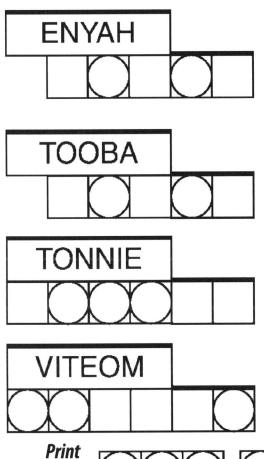

ENYAH

TOOBA

TONNIE

VITEOM

Where did he come from?

THIS CAN TURN A DUET INTO A TRIO.

Now arrange the circled letters to form the surprise answer, as suggested by the above cartoon.

Print answer here

JUMBLE®

Unscramble these four Jumbles, one letter to each square, to form four ordinary words.

NIYKK

GUNEB

VOLJIA

POAFFY

All the better to see you with

HAPPY BIRTHDAY Billy

Those are big

WHEN THE CLOWN WORE THE OUT-RAGEOUS GLASSES, THEY MADE HIM ---

Now arrange the circled letters to form the surprise answer, as suggested by the above cartoon.

Print answer here " ◯◯◯◯ " ◯◯◯◯◯◯

JUMBLE®

Unscramble these four Jumbles, one letter to each square, to form four ordinary words.

BRIHC

NEYOH

YALTIX

GRAULF

Hey! That's mine

No, it's mine

WHAT THE BOWLERS
EXPERIENCED WHEN
THEY ARGUED
OVER THE BALL.

Now arrange the circled letters to form the surprise answer, as suggested by the above cartoon.

Print answer here AN " ◯◯◯◯◯ " ◯◯◯◯◯

119

JUMBLE®

Unscramble these four Jumbles, one letter to each square, to form four ordinary words.

CEROF

EEZSI

SOLUBE

CEXIES

He hasn't won a hand all night

I fold

IT'S THE REVERSE OF SUCCESS.

Now arrange the circled letters to form the surprise answer, as suggested by the above cartoon.

Print answer here

JUMBLE®

Unscramble these four Jumbles, one letter to each square, to form four ordinary words.

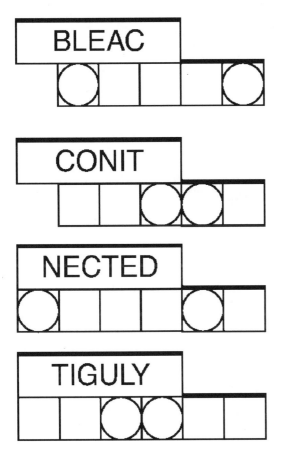

BLEAC

CONIT

NECTED

TIGULY

I always wanted to do this

He's in good shape

WHAT YOU MUST BE TO CLIMB A MOUNTAIN.

Now arrange the circled letters to form the surprise answer, as suggested by the above cartoon.

Print answer here

121

JUMBLE®

Unscramble these four Jumbles, one letter to each square, to form four ordinary words.

ALLIV

OEGOS

CRYPIA

TREFFO

They're so biased

WHAT THE COMMENTATORS' ONE-SIDED VIEWS WERE.

Now arrange the circled letters to form the surprise answer, as suggested by the above cartoon.

Print answer here ⬡⬡⬡⬡⬡⬡⬡⬡⬡

JUMBLE®

Unscramble these four Jumbles, one letter to each square, to form four ordinary words.

RANEY

NOANY

DEGUBB

ACDAFE

...and don't come back!

WHEN THE MUSICIANS GOT TOO WILD, THEY BECAME A ----

Now arrange the circled letters to form the surprise answer, as suggested by the above cartoon.

Print answer here

JUMBLE®

Unscramble these four Jumbles, one letter to
each square, to form four ordinary words.

VOACH

SUJOT

DOXUTE

HUMILE

NEEDED TO AVOID
BITING INSECTS.

Now arrange the circled letters to form the
surprise answer, as suggested by the above
cartoon.

**Print
answer** A
here

124

JUMBLE®

Unscramble these four Jumbles, one letter to
each square, to form four ordinary words.

FLABE

KLEAY

ROWDYS

TAMMOR

Good morning,
Mrs, Smith

WHEN THE PODIATRIST
WENT TO WORK,
IT WAS ---

Now arrange the circled letters to form the
surprise answer, as suggested by the above
cartoon.

**Print
answer
here**

◯◯◯◯◯◯◯ ON " ◯◯◯◯ "

JUMBLE®

Unscramble these four Jumbles, one letter to
each square, to form four ordinary words.

ABISS

RUSUP

LONPEL

GEPPIN

Look straight ahead

WHAT THE SCHOOL
DOCTOR CHECKED
DURING THE
EYE EXAMS.

Now arrange the circled letters to form the
surprise answer, as suggested by the above
cartoon.

Print
answer THE ◯◯◯◯◯◯ ' ◯◯◯◯◯◯
here

JUMBLE®

Unscramble these four Jumbles, one letter to
each square, to form four ordinary words.

VELOH

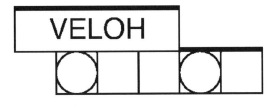

FECAH

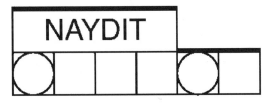

THAAMS

NAYDIT

Aren't you going
to hang them up?

STRIKE ONE!

WHAT HE DID WITH
THE GARDENING
TOOLS WHEN THE
BALL GAME STARTED.

Now arrange the circled letters to form the
surprise answer, as suggested by the above
cartoon.

Print answer here

JUMBLE®

Unscramble these four Jumbles, one letter to
each square, to form four ordinary words.

DENIK

RIVOS

TOXICE

ZAMONA

...and then I heard that Sue...

SHE WENT OVER
FOR SOME SUGAR
AND CAME
HOME WITH ----

Now arrange the circled letters to form the
surprise answer, as suggested by the above
cartoon.

Print answer here ◯◯◯◯ " ◯◯◯◯ "

JUMBLE®

Unscramble these four Jumbles, one letter to
each square, to form four ordinary words.

OSTIC

MIDUH

TOCCUL

YENTIC

Nothing to it.
A couple of
holes and
a buckle

WHAT THE CRAFTS
CLASS SAID WHEN
THEY LEARNED TO
MAKE A BELT.

Now arrange the circled letters to form the
surprise answer, as suggested by the above
cartoon.

*Print answer
here* ⬡⬡ ' ⬡ A " ⬡⬡⬡⬡⬡ "

JUMBLE®

Unscramble these four Jumbles, one letter to
each square, to form four ordinary words.

WOSON

PHACT

YARLIF

KLEECH

The laptop is down

How much gas
do I need?

COMPUTERS AND
RACE CARS HAVE
THIS IN COMMON.

Now arrange the circled letters to form the
surprise answer, as suggested by the above
cartoon.

*Print
answer
here* THEY ◯◯◯ " ◯◯◯◯◯ "

JUMBLE®

Unscramble these four Jumbles, one letter to each square, to form four ordinary words.

GUPER

LUXET

POITTE

PRULAB

What a beautiful night to star gaze

WHAT THE ASTRONOMY CLUB WAS KNOWN AS.

Now arrange the circled letters to form the surprise answer, as suggested by the above cartoon.

Print answer here A " ◯◯◯◯ " ◯◯◯◯◯

JUMBLE®

Unscramble these four Jumbles, one letter to each square, to form four ordinary words.

GLITH

FRAWE

NACAMI

INGALC

I've been on hold for ten minutes

Please stay on the line...

EXPERIENCED BY TELEPHONE USERS.

Now arrange the circled letters to form the surprise answer, as suggested by the above cartoon.

Print answer here

◯◯◯◯ , ◯◯◯◯◯◯◯◯

JUMBLE®

Unscramble these four Jumbles, one letter to each square, to form four ordinary words.

REWFE

LEHEW

ROOMAN

PARREY

I can do the yard in half the time

WHAT THE NEIGHBOR ENJOYED WHEN HE BOUGHT NEW LAWN EQUIPMENT.

Now arrange the circled letters to form the surprise answer, as suggested by the above cartoon.

Print answer here " ◯◯◯◯◯ " ◯◯◯◯◯◯

JUMBLE®

Unscramble these four Jumbles, one letter to each square, to form four ordinary words.

WOPER

YIXST

NAPMEN

BUCHER

Happy Birthday Mom!

One candle is enough

MOM SAID SHE WAS FIFTY, BUT SHE WASN'T ABOUT TO --

Now arrange the circled letters to form the surprise answer, as suggested by the above cartoon.

Print answer here ◯◯◯ ◯◯◯◯

JUMBLE®

Unscramble these four Jumbles, one letter to each square, to form four ordinary words.

RALNS

NOMUD

YGIRLS

NEDDAW

I'm wearing a nice outfit and you're wearing that?

WHAT SHE GAVE HER HUSBAND FOR NOT DRESSING UP.

Now arrange the circled letters to form the surprise answer, as suggested by the above cartoon.

Print answer here A

JUMBLE®

Unscramble these four Jumbles, one letter to each square, to form four ordinary words.

BAIDE

YAFLE

SHUHRT

FINNTA

HOW HE DESCRIBED
HIS NAGGING WIFE.

Now arrange the circled letters to form the
surprise answer, as suggested by the above
cartoon.

Print answer here HIS " ⬡⬡⬡⬡⬡⬡⬡ " ⬡⬡⬡⬡

JUMBLE®

Unscramble these four Jumbles, one letter to
each square, to form four ordinary words.

ENPOY

TOYBO

DRUENE

LISIME

This poem is dedicated
to our new abode

WHAT THE POET
DID WHEN HE BOUGHT
A HOUSE.

Now arrange the circled letters to form the
surprise answer, as suggested by the above
cartoon.

Print answer here " ⬚⬚⬚ " ⬚⬚ ⬚⬚

JUMBLE®

Unscramble these four Jumbles, one letter to
each square, to form four ordinary words.

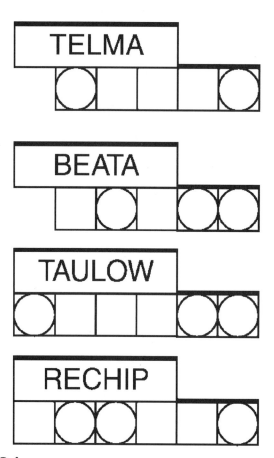

TELMA

BEATA

TAULOW

RECHIP

I hope that they
don't run out of
desserts

EXPERIENCED BY THE
CORPULENT DINER
AT THE END OF A
LONG BUFFET LINE.

Now arrange the circled letters to form the
surprise answer, as suggested by the above
cartoon.

 Print
answer A
here

 " ⬡⬡⬡⬡ "

JUMBLE®

Unscramble these four Jumbles, one letter to
each square, to form four ordinary words.

YADDD

CELER

AMLAMM

BOLGEN

WHAT THE BILL FOR
THE SKIER'S INJURIES
AMOUNTED TO.

Now arrange the circled letters to form the
surprise answer, as suggested by the above
cartoon.

**Print
answer
here** AN ☐◯◯◯ ◯◯◯ A ◯◯◯

JUMBLE

Unscramble these four Jumbles, one letter to
each square, to form four ordinary words.

UPCOE

WONIG

PAWDUR

HYNWIN

It's going to
be close

FINISH LINE

WHEN THE RACING
PIGEONS NEARED THE
FINISH LINE,
IT WAS – – –

Now arrange the circled letters to form the
surprise answer, as suggested by the above
cartoon.

Print answer here ⟨◯◯◯◯⟩ TO THE ⟨◯◯◯◯⟩

JUMBLE®

Unscramble these four Jumbles, one letter to each square, to form four ordinary words.

ADEHA

DEFAM

LURCUN

GIMLEN

This one makes me look slimmer and the other flatters my waistline

...and the price is right

WHAT THE FRUGAL SHOPPER DID WHEN SHE BOUGHT NEW OUTFITS.

Now arrange the circled letters to form the surprise answer, as suggested by the above cartoon.

Print answer here " ◯◯◯◯◯◯◯ "

JUMBLE®

Unscramble these four Jumbles, one letter to each square, to form four ordinary words.

ECIDD

RYKUM

FEEDAC

INFFUM

That's a nice picture of me

WANTED

0217-66-345

WHEN THE BANK
ROBBER SAW HIS
WANTED POSTER,
HE SAID HE WAS ---

Now arrange the circled letters to form the surprise answer, as suggested by the above cartoon.

Print answer here " ⃝⃝⃝⃝⃝⃝⃝ "

JUMBLE®

Unscramble these four Jumbles, one letter to
each square, to form four ordinary words.

GELEY

CRAFS

CLUMON

GLEEBA

They are
centuries old

What
detail

WHAT THE MUSEUM
VISITORS CONSIDERED
THE FAMOUS
SCULPTURES.

Now arrange the circled letters to form the
surprise answer, as suggested by the above
cartoon.

Print
answer
here

"◯◯◯◯◯◯-◯◯◯"

143

JUMBLE®

Unscramble these four Jumbles, one letter to
each square, to form four ordinary words.

SUGET

ANUDT

BLOMIE

SHOMAN

I overslept

WHEN THE CLEANER'S
PRESSER WAS LATE,
THE OWNER WAS ---

Now arrange the circled letters to form the
surprise answer, as suggested by the above
cartoon.

*Print
answer
here*

⬡⬡⬡⬡⬡⬡⬡⬡⬡ , ⬡⬡⬡

JUMBLE®

Unscramble these four Jumbles, one letter to
each square, to form four ordinary words.

MAARD

ORMUF

LIRBED

EUMMUS

That's the third time

What did
you say?

WHAT THE COACH
DID WHEN THE
PLAYER FUMBLED.

Now arrange the circled letters to form the
surprise answer, as suggested by the above
cartoon.

Print answer here

JUMBLE®

Unscramble these four Jumbles, one letter to
each square, to form four ordinary words.

PROUG

CANIP

KEDONY

APHERM

Oh, that's the one.
He's so cute

THEY PICKED THE
DOG WITH THE
WAGGING TAIL
AND HAD A ‒‒‒

Now arrange the circled letters to form the
surprise answer, as suggested by the above
cartoon.

*Print
answer
here*

"

"

JUMBLE®

Unscramble these four Jumbles, one letter to each square, to form four ordinary words.

DAYCE

DOLFO

ROLMAN

YASILE

That's the last batch. I'm going home

WHAT THE HARD-WORKING BAKER DID.

Now arrange the circled letters to form the surprise answer, as suggested by the above cartoon.

Print answer here " ◯◯◯◯◯◯ " ALL ◯◯◯

JUMBLE®

Unscramble these four Jumbles, one letter to
each square, to form four ordinary words.

UFORR

RYDYL

SWEENT

PHUDEL

Mine make a
whistling sound

Mine click

CAN BE HEARD WITH
FALSE TEETH.

Now arrange the circled letters to form the
surprise answer, as suggested by the above
cartoon.

Print answer here

JUMBLE®

Unscramble these four Jumbles, one letter to
each square, to form four ordinary words.

ROBEW

PAUNC

BURPES

GROJAN

WHAT THE DRIVER
DID IN THE
DEMOLITION RACE.

Now arrange the circled letters to form the
surprise answer, as suggested by the above
cartoon.

Print
answer A "◯◯◯◯◯ ◯◯" ◯◯◯
here

149

JUMBLE®

Unscramble these four Jumbles, one letter to each square, to form four ordinary words.

DOPEK

VALEE

TONPHY

LUNIKE

I'm so nervous

This one opens cells and this one...

WHEN THE NEW PRISON GUARD WENT ON DUTY, HE WAS ---

Now arrange the circled letters to form the surprise answer, as suggested by the above cartoon.

Print answer here " ☐☐☐☐☐ " ☐☐

JUMBLE®

Unscramble these four Jumbles, one letter to
each square, to form four ordinary words.

PYKER

ZIMEA

MENECT

SYTTUR

This is your
last chance

WHAT THE COSME-
TOLOGY STUDENT
FACED WHEN SHE
MISSED THE EXAM.

Now arrange the circled letters to form the
surprise answer, as suggested by the above
cartoon.

**Print
answer
here** A " ◯◯◯◯◯◯ " ◯◯◯◯

JUMBLE®

Unscramble these four Jumbles, one letter to each square, to form four ordinary words.

NEFIT

NIROY

AKCEPT

WHARTT

I have all these ideas in my head

WHEN THE RUNNER DECIDED TO BECOME A NOVELIST, HE WAS ON ----

Now arrange the circled letters to form the surprise answer, as suggested by the above cartoon.

Print answer here THE " ◯◯◯◯◯ " ◯◯◯◯◯

JUMBLE®

Unscramble these four Jumbles, one letter to
each square, to form four ordinary words.

GELBI

YASTT

ZEEWEH

GEDDER

I'll have updates
every ten minutes

WHAT THE
FORECASTER DID
WHEN THE STRONG
STORM APPROACHED.

Now arrange the circled letters to form the
surprise answer, as suggested by the above
cartoon.

*Print
answer
here*   "⟨ ⟩⟨ ⟩⟨ ⟩⟨ ⟩⟨ ⟩⟨ ⟩⟨ ⟩⟨ ⟩⟨ ⟩⟨ ⟩" ⟨ ⟩⟨ ⟩

JUMBLE®

Unscramble these four Jumbles, one letter to each square, to form four ordinary words.

CALVO

OSPOT

PERTAT

BLUHME

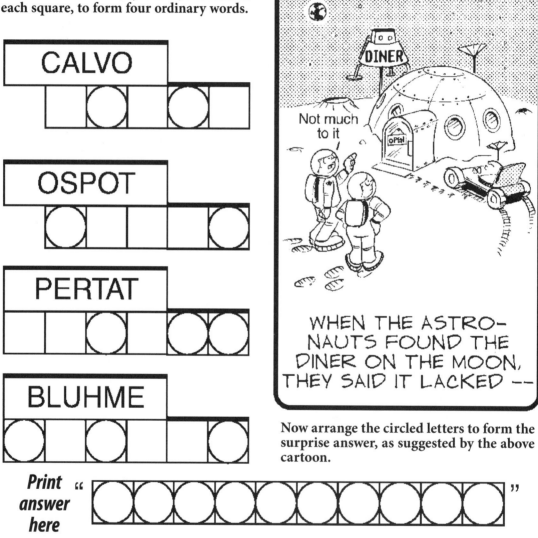

Not much to it

DINER

OPEN

WHEN THE ASTRO-
NAUTS FOUND THE
DINER ON THE MOON,
THEY SAID IT LACKED --

Now arrange the circled letters to form the surprise answer, as suggested by the above cartoon.

Print answer here " ◯◯◯◯◯◯◯◯◯◯ "

JUMBLE®

Unscramble these four Jumbles, one letter to each square, to form four ordinary words.

PULIT

BAZLE

NAUTER

HOYTER

Your are the best

We'll help clean up

Flour

A GOOD WAY TO GET MOM TO MAKE THEIR FAVORITE COOKIES.

Now arrange the circled letters to form the surprise answer, as suggested by the above cartoon.

Print answer here "  "

JUMBLE®

Unscramble these four Jumbles, one letter to
each square, to form four ordinary words.

GAGBY

UTOOD

SERBIC

LADHER

This is Beaver
ACHOO!
The dawn has burst

WHY THE SPY
TALKED FUNNY.

Now arrange the circled letters to form the
surprise answer, as suggested by the above
cartoon.

**Print answer
here**   HE ⬡⬡⬡ A " ⬡⬡⬡⬡ "

JUMBLE®

Unscramble these four Jumbles, one letter to each square, to form four ordinary words.

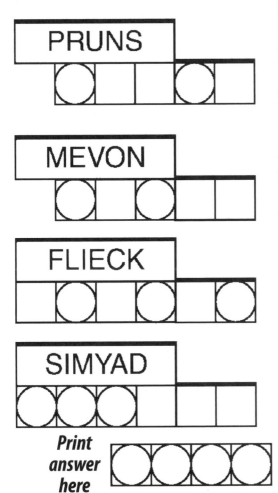

PRUNS

MEVON

FLIECK

SIMYAD

I'm getting bit

Me, too

WHAT THE MOSQUITOES TURNED INTO WHEN THEY SPOTTED THE BEACH PARTY.

Now arrange the circled letters to form the surprise answer, as suggested by the above cartoon.

Print answer here

JUMBLE®

Unscramble these four Jumbles, one letter to
each square, to form four ordinary words.

TILAP

JONEY

ENSICC

DAGAPO

Pay attention.
Do exactly as
I say

WHAT THE
BALLERINAS DID
AT THE AUDITION.

Now arrange the circled letters to form the
surprise answer, as suggested by the above
cartoon.

Print
answer
here " ◯◯◯◯ " THE ◯◯◯◯

JUMBLE®

Unscramble these four Jumbles, one letter to
each square, to form four ordinary words.

GULIE

GLUNE

HINGKT

WARIAY

It still works

DONG

DONG

WHEN THE SAILORS
RETRIEVED THE
SHIP'S BELL,
IT WAS ----

Now arrange the circled letters to form the
surprise answer, as suggested by the above
cartoon.

Print
answer
here   " ⃝⃝⃝⃝⃝⃝⃝ " ⃝⃝⃝

JUMBLE®

Unscramble these four Jumbles, one letter to
each square, to form four ordinary words.

DONEM

NOYOL

CROONB

LAFICA

Not a cent for
a year, Your Honor

You got
everything

LACK OF ALIMONY
CAN RESULT IN THIS.

Now arrange the circled letters to form the
surprise answer, as suggested by the above
cartoon.

Print answer here

JUMBLE®

Unscramble these four Jumbles, one letter to
each square, to form four ordinary words.

FRIGE

GADEA

SHOMID

MEESID

Two scrambled, one over easy,
three sunnyside. C'mon, you're falling behind

WHAT THE WAITRESS
DID TO THE SHORT
ORDER COOK.

Now arrange the circled letters to form the
surprise answer, as suggested by the above
cartoon.

Print
answer
here   " ◯◯◯◯◯ " ◯◯◯ ON

JUMBLE®

Unscramble these four Jumbles, one letter to each square, to form four ordinary words.

KWISH

KROPE

LEWVIE

PRAULL

AN IMPORTANT EXERCISE FOR A DIETER.

Now arrange the circled letters to form the surprise answer, as suggested by the above cartoon.

Print answer here

JUMBLE

Sensation

Challenger Puzzles

JUMBLE®

Unscramble these six Jumbles, one letter to
each square, to form six ordinary words.

HIRTTY

UNPOCE

SOPPEO

SOUBLE

CYSTOL

YAFFOP

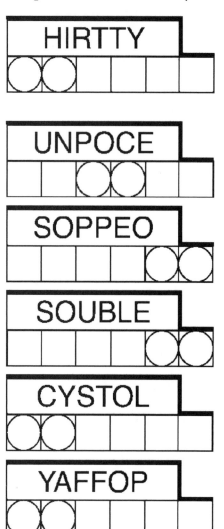

His prints
are all over
the evidence

WHEN THE DOOR-
MAN WAS ARRESTED,
THE DETECTIVE SAID
IT WAS AN---

Now arrange the circled letters to form the
surprise answer, as suggested by the above
cartoon.

Print answer here

AND

JUMBLE®

Unscramble these six Jumbles, one letter to each square, to form six ordinary words.

BROMEY

GOFTER

EMSIDE

LESCUM

LEWOLF

MEAPER

I need a shirt ironed

I've got a deadline. You do it

WHAT THE REPORTER DEMANDED WHEN THE IRONING PILED UP.

Now arrange the circled letters to form the surprise answer, as suggested by the above cartoon.

Print answer here

◯◯◯◯◯◯◯ OF THE " ◯◯◯◯◯ "

JUMBLE®

Unscramble these six Jumbles, one letter to each square, to form six ordinary words.

PERMAC

INSLUM

SHATAM

INGUSE

LUMEFF

VAJILO

He was so friendly and polite

BANK

THE WELL-MANNERED COUNTERFEITER GAVE THE BANK TELLER A----

Now arrange the circled letters to form the surprise answer, as suggested by the above cartoon.

Print answer here

◯◯◯◯◯ " ◯◯◯◯◯◯◯◯◯◯ "

JUMBLE®

Unscramble these six Jumbles, one letter to
each square, to form six ordinary words.

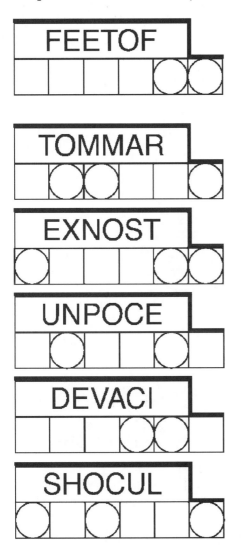

FEETOF

TOMMAR

EXNOST

UNPOCE

DEVACI

SHOCUL

Oh, it came
out perfect

WHEN THE HOSTESS
BAKED HER OWN
BREAD FOR THE
PARTY, IT---

Now arrange the circled letters to form the
surprise answer, as suggested by the above
cartoon.

Print answer here

TO

JUMBLE

Unscramble these six Jumbles, one letter to
each square, to form six ordinary words.

CRUSHO

INGUSE

CIPTED

THACAT

DELTUC

HIRTTY

I can't get a steady aim

WHAT THE HUNTERS
DID IN THE
SWIRLING RIVER.

Now arrange the circled letters to form the
surprise answer, as suggested by the above
cartoon.

Print answer here

JUMBLE®

Unscramble these six Jumbles, one letter to
each square, to form six ordinary words.

DRIBHY

SOPPEO

TELRUT

BEMUND

AMLAMM

DOLFYN

It's out of
control. More
guards are
on the way

HOW THE NEWSMAN
DESCRIBED THE
PRISON UPRISING.

Now arrange the circled letters to form the
surprise answer, as suggested by the above
cartoon.

Print answer here

" ◯◯◯ - ◯◯◯◯◯◯◯◯ "

JUMBLE.

Unscramble these six Jumbles, one letter to each square, to form six ordinary words.

COPTEK

VAJILO

UNGOTE

KAMBER

CYSTOL

LYROOP

Those screwballs can't agree on anything

Needs salt

Absolutely not

WHY THE CHEFS COULDN'T MAKE A GOOD SOUP.

Now arrange the circled letters to form the surprise answer, as suggested by the above cartoon.

Print answer here

JUMBLE®

Unscramble these six Jumbles, one letter to
each square, to form six ordinary words.

NAWDDE

GUTHAT

TYBLUS

RESAIT

NARTOM

TERVOX

Wow! I was here only
a couple of minutes

WHAT SHE CONSID-
ERED THE SKIN
DOCTOR'S BILL.

Now arrange the circled letters to form the
surprise answer, as suggested by the above
cartoon.

Print answer here

A ⬡⬡⬡⬡ " ⬡⬡⬡⬡⬡⬡⬡⬡⬡⬡ "

JUMBLE®

Unscramble these six Jumbles, one letter to
each square, to form six ordinary words.

EMBOCE

HILUME

OVVEEL

TRAMOF

LUDSON

ULDDEC

This isn't the latest

But it fits
you perfectly

WHEN THE FASHION
PLATE WENT
SHOPPING, SHE
WAS---

Now arrange the circled letters to form the
surprise answer, as suggested by the above
cartoon.

Print answer here

" ◯◯◯◯◯◯◯◯ " ◯◯◯◯◯◯

JUMBLE®

Unscramble these six Jumbles, one letter to each square, to form six ordinary words.

GRUHNY

VIYTLE

LERVAM

MLUEHB

FEECAD

CUPHAN

Tickets, please

Nice fight, Butch

WHAT THE CON-
DUCTOR DID WHEN
THE CHAMP RODE
THE TRAIN.

Now arrange the circled letters to form the surprise answer, as suggested by the above cartoon.

Print answer here

☐☐☐☐ ☐☐☐ A " ☐☐☐☐☐ "

173

JUMBLE®

Unscramble these six Jumbles, one letter to each square, to form six ordinary words.

WARBOR

NOBARC

CHENIL

NAPHOR

FIVERD

ONASAT

I run the west side office and have my own secretary

WHEN THE TREE CUTTER WAS PRO-MOTED, HE HAD----

Now arrange the circled letters to form the surprise answer, as suggested by the above cartoon.

Print answer here

174

JUMBLE®

Unscramble these six Jumbles, one letter to each square, to form six ordinary words.

GASYRS

GERDED

KLEFIC

PELETS

MIDYOF

FISHET

You're straining. These new glasses should help

E

WHAT HE CONSID-
ERED THE OPTOME-
TRIST'S OFFICE.

Now arrange the circled letters to form the surprise answer, as suggested by the above cartoon.

Print answer here

A ⬡⬡⬡⬡⬡ FOR ⬡⬡⬡⬡⬡ ⬡⬡⬡⬡⬡

175

JUMBLE®

Unscramble these six Jumbles, one letter to
each square, to form six ordinary words.

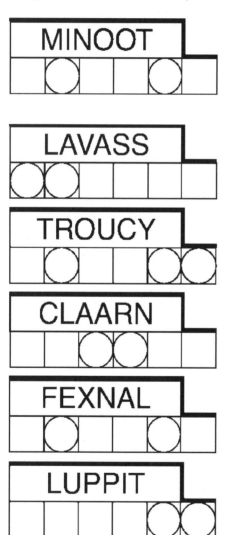

MINOOT

LAVASS

TROUCY

CLAARN

FEXNAL

LUPPIT

It's stopping

It needs
to be
cranked

WHEN RECORD
PLAYERS FIRST
APPEARED, THEY
WERE----

Now arrange the circled letters to form the
surprise answer, as suggested by the above
cartoon.

Print answer here

" "

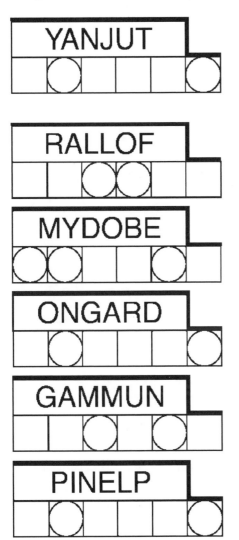

JUMBLE®

Unscramble these six Jumbles, one letter to each square, to form six ordinary words.

YANJUT

RALLOF

MYDOBE

ONGARD

GAMMUN

PINELP

Want to go to the movies tomorrow?

WHEN THE SLEEP THERAPIST ASKED HER OUT, SHE SAID---

Now arrange the circled letters to form the surprise answer, as suggested by the above cartoon.

Print answer here

177

JUMBLE®

Unscramble these six Jumbles, one letter to each square, to form six ordinary words.

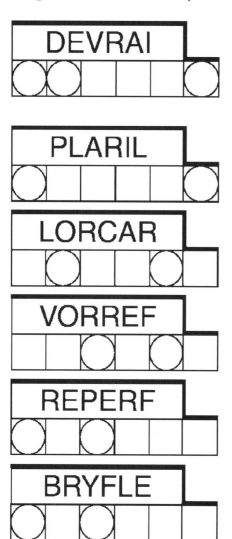

DEVRAI

PLARIL

LORCAR

VORREF

REPERF

BRYFLE

Do you agree?

Yeah, sure
Go ahead

Why not?

WHAT THE DIREC-
TORS GAVE THE
COMPANY PRESI-
DENT'S PLAN---

Now arrange the circled letters to form the surprise answer, as suggested by the above cartoon.

Print answer here

" ⬡⬡⬡⬡⬡ " ⬡⬡⬡⬡⬡⬡⬡⬡

JUMBLE®

Unscramble these six Jumbles, one letter to each square, to form six ordinary words.

REMIPE

MACEEB

WYIHNN

HANKES

LINCEY

GORFTO

WHEN THE MARRIED MIMES LEFT FOR WORK, THEY----

Now arrange the circled letters to form the surprise answer, as suggested by the above cartoon.

Print answer here

JUMBLE®

Unscramble these six Jumbles, one letter to each square, to form six ordinary words.

STURME

TRARAT

ROVACT

SPEBIC

GOEMAH

CAFUTE

I worked in the mail room while getting my master's

A GOOD WAY TO CLIMB THE LADDER OF SUCCESS.

Now arrange the circled letters to form the surprise answer, as suggested by the above cartoon.

Print answer here

◯◯◯◯◯◯ AT ◯◯◯◯ ◯◯◯◯◯◯◯

JUMBLE®

Unscramble these six Jumbles, one letter to
each square, to form six ordinary words.

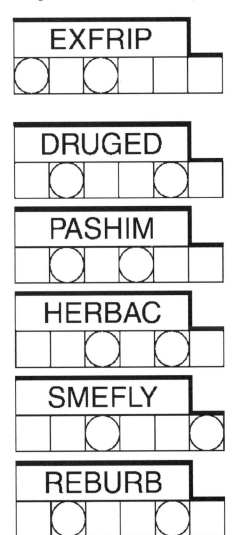

EXFRIP

DRUGED

PASHIM

HERBAC

SMEFLY

REBURB

...and to all my fans,
I'd like to say...

THE BEAUTY
QUEEN TURNED
INTO THIS WHEN
SHE ADDRESSED
THE CROWD.

Now arrange the circled letters to form the
surprise answer, as suggested by the above
cartoon.

Print answer here

A " ⬭⬭⬭⬭⬭⬭ " OF ⬭⬭⬭⬭⬭⬭

JUMBLE®

Unscramble these six Jumbles, one letter to
each square, to form six ordinary words.

PARTIE

OOGLYD

UNMAUT

GINTHK

TRIMOP

MEUGLE

I'll have
another

Oops, I
missed a
loop

WHEN THE HOSTESS
SERVED COCKTAILS,
THE CROCHET CLUB
BECAME A ----

Now arrange the circled letters to form the
surprise answer, as suggested by the above
cartoon.

Print answer here

" ⃝⃝⃝⃝⃝ " ⃝⃝⃝⃝ ⃝⃝⃝⃝⃝

JUMBLE®

Unscramble these six Jumbles, one letter to each square, to form six ordinary words.

WHEENP

CENTIE

LAPLID

YONKED

INDOWS

HALEXE

LET CURVEBALL CAL SELL YOU A CAR

You'll enjoy this beauty

THE STRIKEOUT ARTIST WENT INTO SALES BECAUSE HE---

Now arrange the circled letters to form the surprise answer, as suggested by the above cartoon.

Print answer here

◯◯◯◯◯ ◯◯◯ TO " ◯◯◯◯◯◯ "

Answers

1. **Jumbles:** LUSTY MOUSY FLUNKY ADRIFT
   Answer: What the newlyweds considered their checking account—A "MUTUAL" FUND

2. **Jumbles:** MINER OBESE SAVORY GOSPEL
   Answer: Learning how to drive can lead to this—SOME "REVERSES"

3. **Jumbles:** MOTIF IDIOM BEYOND UNEASY
   Answer: When the roommates studied anatomy, they knew their subject—INSIDE OUT

4. **Jumbles:** CHAMP AUDIT OCCULT SLOGAN
   Answer: She decided to go out with the outfielder because he was—A GOOD "CATCH"

5. **Jumbles:** CRUSH SOUSE PARADE DELUXE
   Answer: When the newspaper closed, the workers were—"DE-PRESSED"

6. **Jumbles:** FLUID GRAVE TYPHUS HITHER
   Answer: Why the sultry singer got the business outfit—IT "SUITED" HER

7. **Jumbles:** DRAMA BILGE GIBLET LEAVEN
   Answer: When the candidates discussed the issues, their views were—"DEBATABLE"

8. **Jumbles:** THYME FAMED SCRIBE BOYISH
   Answer: What he improved when he jogged—HIS MEMORY

9. **Jumbles:** VOCAL PARCH MALADY GOITER
   Answer: When the do-it-yourselfer summoned a plumber, he made—THE RIGHT "CALL"

10. **Jumbles:** ENJOY IRONY DOUBLE HIATUS
    Answer: What the commuters did when the train finally arrived—THEY "RAILED"

11. **Jumbles:** FLUKE SILKY LAWYER JACKET
    Answer: How she felt after the fender bender—LIKE A "WRECK"

12. **Jumbles:** VALVE OZONE FACIAL GLANCE
    Answer: What the shepherd got when he took his herd to market—A "FLEECING"

13. **Jumbles:** TARDY PRIOR NUMBER MELODY
    Answer: What the tailors finally did when they both needed to press pants—"IRONED" IT OUT

14. **Jumbles:** RABBI ALIAS ROSARY PYTHON
    Answer: They enjoy discussing old times at a reunion—HISTORIANS

15. **Jumbles:** LISLE BERET TORRID GYRATE
    Answer: The postal clerk was good at solving anagrams because he was a—LETTER SORTER

16. **Jumbles:** ARRAY LIMIT COUPON BOUNCE
    Answer: When the gardener spotted the dying shrub, he got to the—"ROOT" OF THE PROBLEM

17. **Jumbles:** GROUP PERKY LIQUID THRESH
    Answer: When the tipsy sailor was saved from falling overboard, he was—HIGH AND DRY

18. **Jumbles:** JETTY CHANT MARTYR BEETLE
    Answer: Enjoyed by lovebirds on Valentine's Day—A "HEARTY" MEAL

19. **Jumbles:** VOUCH UTTER DURESS JOSTLE
    Answer: The army barber took this to save time—SHORT CUTS

20. **Jumbles:** CREEK QUILT POETRY CAMPUS
    Answer: When the locksmith got the high-rise job, the builder became his—"KEY" CUSTOMER

21. **Jumbles:** ADULT FEWER CLOTHE AVENUE
    Answer: They lauded the astronaut because he was—DOWN TO "EARTH"

22. **Jumbles:** BRIAR STOOP EMPLOY GOATEE
    Answer: When the pianist played the new piece, he found it was—"TREBLE-SOME"

23. **Jumbles:** FLUTE TWILL EFFIGY BLAZER
    Answer: His claim of losing 100 pounds turned out to be—A BIG "FAT" LIE

24. **Jumbles:** LUNGE COUGH HAMPER CATNIP
    Answer: The teen left his clothes on the floor because he had a—HANG UP HANG-UP

25. **Jumbles:** UNWED FATAL STYMIE ARTFUL
    Answer: What happened when she spelled the word right—SHE WAS "LEFT"

26. **Jumbles:** SOAPY WALTZ PARODY COLUMN
    Answer: When the brothers' pillow fight ended, it was—"DOWN" AND OUT

27. **Jumbles:** TULIP POACH UPHELD SCROLL
    Answer: What the divorced father gave his son—CHILD "SUPPORT"

28. **Jumbles:** VITAL MOUNT PERSON SPLICE
    Answer: Trying to sew with a broken needle is—"POINTLESS"

29. **Jumbles:** HONOR BOUGH FOURTH ORIGIN
    Answer: How the pig farmer ended up living when he sold out—HIGH ON THE "HOG"

30. **Jumbles:** LINEN CROON OBTUSE JAGGED
    Answer: What the successful deep-sea diver never worries about—GOING "UNDER"

31. **Jumbles:** LEECH POKED ALKALI WALNUT
    Answer: What the late-arriving guest gave the night clerk—A "WAKE-UP" CALL

32. **Jumbles:** BISON AGLOW CALMLY CANINE
    Answer: Why she became an operator—IT WAS A "CALLING"

33. **Jumbles:** GLORY NEEDY ARMADA PLAQUE
    Answer: When the cyclers completed the hill climb, they—MADE THE "GRADE"

34. **Jumbles:** INEPT OPERA JARGON PLACID
    Answer: He played soccer because he was—"GOAL" ORIENTED

35. **Jumbles:** KITTY ANNUL MODISH JITNEY
    Answer: Often goes along with a thick body—A THIN SKIN

36. **Jumbles:** BATCH WHILE UTMOST SLEIGH
    Answer: What the hostess said when her guests brought dessert—THAT'S SO "SWEET"

37. **Jumbles:** FLAME ACRID THROAT BASKET
    Answer: Giving kids household duties can be a—CHORE IN ITSELF

38. **Jumbles:** GIVEN MANLY BEHOLD HAIRDO
    Answer: What the little old clockmaker's helper did—GAVE HIM A "HAND"

39. **Jumbles:** NOOSE SURLY TOUCHY FROLIC
    Answer: Why the sports cameraman was fired—HE LOST HIS "FOCUS"

40. **Jumbles:** NUTTY FLORA EXODUS OFFSET
    Answer: Usually found at a taxidermy shop—LOTS OF "STUFF"

41. **Jumbles:** CLOAK BELLE PUDDLE NOUGAT
    Answer: What the twins gave Mom when the lamp fell—"DOUBLE" TALK

42. **Jumbles:** FRIAR POPPY BALSAM BUMPER
    Answer: Sound right, but very wrong, to cross a flooded street—A PAIR OF "PUMPS"

43. **Jumbles:** SCARY LIMBO BELLOW LEDGER
    Answer: What happened when he came home stewed—HE WAS "GRILLED"

44. **Jumbles:** OPIUM BARGE PANTRY UNSEAT
    Answer: How the harpist felt when the recital ended—"STRUNG" OUT

45. **Jumbles:** ABHOR VAPOR BEACON EMERGE
    Answer: What the hosts wished their guests would do—GO HOME

46. **Jumbles:** GORGE WHINE FOIBLE TRIBAL
    Answer: When the servers didn't get along, there was a—FIGHT "BREWING"

47. **Jumbles:** PRIME STUNG BALLET FIESTA
    Answer: How the coach described the tired sprinter—FAST, ASLEEP

48. **Jumbles:** CHUTE DEMON MATURE PELVIS
Answer: Why the yoga instructor didn't answer the phone—HE WAS "TIED UP"

49. **Jumbles:** MESSY PRUNE OPAQUE ACTUAL
Answer: What the foreman wanted the lazy carpenter to do—"STEP" IT UP

50. **Jumbles:** OCCUR BOWER AFLOAT UNCLAD
Answer: Why the king went to the dentist—FOR A "CROWN"

51. **Jumbles:** DITTY ARDOR MORBID HANGAR
Answer: What the unhappy customers gave the beauty shop owner—A BAD HAIR DAY

52. **Jumbles:** TAFFY HUMAN PARDON THWART
Answer: Deep sea diving can be this—HARD TO "FATHOM"

53. **Jumbles:** IDIOT WEDGE BANANA AWHILE
Answer: What the watchmaker decided to do as he got on in years—"WIND" DOWN

54. **Jumbles:** LEGAL GAUZE TYPING GARLIC
Answer: He helped his wife clean the vegetables and found the task—A-PEELING

55. **Jumbles:** ROUSE CANAL DILUTE WOEFUL
Answer: What a successful dentist does—"FILLS" A NEED

56. **Jumbles:** SPURN HIKER KITTEN QUAINT
Answer: The first thing a teenager will do—TURN THIRTEEN

57. **Jumbles:** GUMBO APART KOSHER DETACH
Answer: What the umbrella salesman did during the rainstorm—HE "SOAKED" THEM

58. **Jumbles:** ACUTE RIVET COUSIN UNCOIL
Answer: When he did a poor job installing the window treatment, it was—"CURTAINS"

59. **Jumbles:** ERUPT THICK LADING PURITY
Answer: What the bowler used when his ball went astray—"GUTTER" TALK

60. **Jumbles:** DAUNT STEED WHITEN EULOGY
Answer: Why the baker didn't make much money—HE WASTED HIS "DOUGH"

61. **Jumbles:** FAINT ROACH HECTIC MARMOT
Answer: When they met on the tennis court and later married, it was a—MATCH MATCH

62. **Jumbles:** DUSKY VIPER FEEBLE SLOUCH
Answer: What the beauticians did before the cosmetics exam—"BRUSHED" UP

63. **Jumbles:** VIRUS SIEGE ANSWER FIASCO
Answer: Easily raised at morning roll call—SARGE'S VOICE

64. **Jumbles:** EXULT HOIST DEPUTY NEEDLE
Answer: What the hotel guest did before he settled down for the night—SETTLED UP

65. **Jumbles:** FANCY DIRTY POETIC CANOPY
Answer: Passing his driver's test was—NO "ACCIDENT"

66. **Jumbles:** BRAWL HYENA PONDER BOILED
Answer: What the farmboy did on the football field—"PLOWED" AHEAD

67. **Jumbles:** FRUIT IMPEL TIMING AGENCY
Answer: When the scouts had a knot-making contest, it turned into a—"TIE" GAME

68. **Jumbles:** SWASH FINAL MOTIVE GOLFER
Answer: What the scientists decided to do when they studied the icebergs—GO WITH THE "FLOE"

69. **Jumbles:** MOUTH ROBIN TAMPER DEMURE
Answer: When the class got rowdy, the math teacher did a—"NUMBER" ON THEM

70. **Jumbles:** HELLO ODDLY POLLEN DAMAGE
Answer: What the greyhound turned into when he raced around the track—A "LAP" DOG

71. **Jumbles:** WAGER FORCE BEHAVE QUARRY
Answer: When he got a dead battery from the junkyard, it was—FREE OF "CHARGE"

72. **Jumbles:** HONEY CAKED FAIRLY PIRACY
Answer: A nice welcome—"CORDIAL"

73. **Jumbles:** HANDY TAWNY REDUC E MYOPIC
Answer: When the gangster went to prison, he became part of—THE "IN" CROWD

74. **Jumbles:** DROOP VILLA EXEMPT PRISON
Answer: This can happen to "models"—"SELDOM"

75. **Jumbles:** CABLE FORTY OUTING LAGOON
Answer: What she got from her new hairstyle—A "BANG" OUT OF IT

76. **Jumbles:** GUILE ABATE EQUITY OFFSET
Answer: When the young lad tried on the tailored suit, Mom had a—FIT FIT

77. **Jumbles:** HAZEL LOUSY DUPLEX BODICE
Answer: Not a good way to pick a friend—TO PIECES

78. **Jumbles:** HENNA MIDGE WAITER DRAGON
Answer: When he was late for their beach date, she was—DONE "WADING"

79. **Jumbles:** EXACT KETCH SMOKER PRAYER
Answer: What the farmer experienced when he began building a stone wall—A "ROCKY" START

80. **Jumbles:** BULLY GRIEF INDOOR AIRWAY
Answer: When the problem was difficult to solve, the student saved it for a—"BRAINY" DAY

81. **Jumbles:** DINER PATIO PERSON CAMPUS
Answer: Shared by a flower stem and a florist shop—MEANS OF SUPPORT

82. **Jumbles:** STOKE CLOVE MIDDAY PULPIT
Answer: When he returned to his old hangout, he paid—A VISIT

83. **Jumbles:** AGLOW BOWER FORCED DISARM
Answer: What the artist and the smash hit musical had in common—THEY "DREW" CROWDS

84. **Jumbles:** OUTDO STOOP GASKET CARBON
Answer: Her fiancé was quite a catch because he came from—GOOD "STOCK"

85. **Jumbles:** ARRAY RHYME FICKLE LIQUID
Answer: Used by a banker to make a point—A DECIMAL

86. **Jumbles:** CHEEK ADAGE UNLIKE FABLED
Answer: When the baker had an idea for a new cake, it turned out to be—HALF-BAKED

87. **Jumbles:** GUARD BARGE FERVOR SCHOOL
Answer: What the insurance agent's daughter got when he tucked her in—GOOD "COVERAGE"

88. **Jumbles:** FORUM POUCH RAMROD PACKET
Answer: What the doctor did when the ailing actor overreacted—CURED THE "HAM"

89. **Jumbles:** LOGIC GIANT UPKEEP PUMICE
Answer: With the economy down, the garbage collector said business was—PICKING UP

90. **Jumbles:** GAMUT LADLE FERVID PARODY
Answer: When her husband wanted to take a hot-air balloon ride, he—"FLOATED" THE IDEA

91. **Jumbles:** WIPED VENOM PROFIT DETAIN
Answer: "Lefty" joined the school newspaper because he was—"WRITE" MINDED

92. **Jumbles:** GLADE DAISY JOSTLE PENURY
Answer: The teen did the wash because it was part of her—"LAUNDRY" LIST

93. **Jumbles:** BRAVE GUESS PELVIS SURETY
Answer: What the boxers exchanged before the big fight—VERSUS VERSES

94. **Jumbles:** SAUTE CHAIR EQUATE DEVOUR
Answer: When the general went to bed, his pillow became his—HEAD "QUARTERS"

95. **Jumbles:** WHEAT POKER FOURTH DOUBLY
Answer: What the bathers did when they hit the burning sand—"HOT FOOTED" IT

96. **Jumbles:** MONEY LINER INWARD FACING
Answer: Today a cell phone can do this—RING IN THE NEW YEAR

97. **Jumbles:** TAWNY VYING JUGGLE PALACE
Answer: When the stagehand couldn't get the lights to work, he kept—"PLUGGING" AWAY

185

98. **Jumbles:** STAID FETID OBLONG QUEASY
Answer: The trombonist joined the marching band because he knew the—INS AND OUTS

99. **Jumbles:** FOIST CROAK MORTAR PETITE
Answer: What the overweight sunbather experienced at the beach—A "POT" ROAST

100. **Jumbles:** JUROR CYCLE JUMBLE FINISH
Answer: A good way to keep your age—TO YOURSELF

101. **Jumbles:** CUBIC EXTOL SAVAGE CAUCUS
Answer: What the did when he left for the office—GOT THE "BUSS"

102. **Jumbles:** SWAMP BERTH OPIATE HAGGLE
Answer: How he kept their bills down—A PAPERWEIGHT

103. **Jumbles:** WAGER HOIST INVOKE KOWTOW
Answer: What she lost on the 14-day diet—TWO WEEKS

104. **Jumbles:** WOMEN DRONE BOUGHT FIASCO
Answer: A common way to start out when learning to dance—ON THE WRONG FOOT

105. **Jumbles:** DITTO CHALK SALOON VACUUM
Answer: What he needed to heat his house—"COLD" CASH

106. **Jumbles:** GRIPE BUSHY ACCENT FAMILY
Answer: Usually last for years on new cars—PAYMENTS

107. **Jumbles:** JUICY BIPED BABOON JUNKET
Answer: When the salesman ate at the seafood restaurant, he had a—BONE TO PICK

108. **Jumbles:** APPLY MOUTH BUBBLE FAMISH
Answer: What the accident victim got for the bump on his head—A "LUMP" SUM

109. **Jumbles:** SIEGE LOFTY SIPHON ENCAMP
Answer: An unsharpened pencil is this—POINTLESS

110. **Jumbles:** LURID KHAKI ARCADE SEXTON
Answer: What the ladies did when they cleaned the office—SHARED THE "DIRT"

111. **Jumbles:** CLOTH BRAVO AVOWAL QUORUM
Answer: When the tire dealers held their dance, it turned into a—"BLOWOUT"

112. **Jumbles:** HELLO SCOUT COERCE SCURVY
Answer: What the football team achieved when they won 20-0—A SCORE SCORE

113. **Jumbles:** ROBIN DIRTY BOILED FABRIC
Answer: When he wore the outdated corduroys, he was—"RIBBED"

114. **Jumbles:** FUDGE EJECT MURMUR VICUNA
Answer: What he faced when he worked at the cemetery—A "GRAVE" FUTURE

115. **Jumbles:** HYENA TABOO INTONE MOTIVE
Answer: This can turn a duet into a trio—ONE TOO MANY

116. **Jumbles:** KINKY BEGUN JOVIAL PAYOFF
Answer: When the clown wore the outrageous glasses, they made him—"LOOK" FUNNY

117. **Jumbles:** BIRCH HONEY LAXITY FRUGAL
Answer: What the bowlers experienced when they argued over the ball—AN "ALLEY" FIGHT

118. **Jumbles:** FORCE SEIZE BLOUSE EXCISE
Answer: It's the reverse of success—SSECCUS

119. **Jumbles:** CABLE TONIC DECENT GUILTY
Answer: What you must be to climb a mountain—"INCLINED"

120. **Jumbles:** VILLA GOOSE PIRACY EFFORT
Answer: What the commentators' one-sided views were—PROFILES

121. **Jumbles:** YEARN ANNOY BEDBUG FACADE
Answer: When the musicians got too wild, they became a—BANNED BAND

122. **Jumbles:** HAVOC JOUST TUXEDO HELIUM
Answer: Needed to avoid biting insects—A CLOSED MOUTH

123. **Jumbles:** FABLE LEAKY DROWSY MARMOT
Answer: When the podiatrist went to work, it was—ALWAYS ON "FOOT"

124. **Jumbles:** BASIS USURP POLLEN PIGPEN
Answer: What the school doctor checked during the eye exams—THE PUPILS' PUPILS

125. **Jumbles:** HOVEL CHAFE ASTHMA DAINTY
Answer: What he did with the gardening tools when the ball game started—"SHED" THEM

126. **Jumbles:** INKED VISOR EXOTIC AMAZON
Answer: She went over for some sugar and came home with—SOME "DIRT"

127. **Jumbles:** STOIC HUMID OCCULT NICETY
Answer: What the crafts class said when they learned to make a belt—IT'S A "CINCH"

128. **Jumbles:** SWOON PATCH FAIRLY HECKLE
Answer: Computers and race cars have this in common—THEY CAN "CRASH"

129. **Jumbles:** PURGE EXULT TIPTOE BURLAP
Answer: What the astronomy club was known as—A "PEER" GROUP

130. **Jumbles:** LIGHT WAFER MANIAC LACING
Answer: Experienced by telephone users—CALL, WAITING

131. **Jumbles:** FEWER WHEEL MAROON PRAYER
Answer: What the neighbor enjoyed when he bought new lawn equipment—"MOWER" POWER

132. **Jumbles:** POWER SIXTY PENMAN CHERUB
Answer: Mom said she was fifty, but she wasn't about to—SAY WHEN

133. **Jumbles:** SNARL MOUND GRISLY DAWNED
Answer: What she gave her husband for not dressing up—A DRESSING DOWN

134. **Jumbles:** ABIDE LEAFY THRUSH INFANT
Answer: How he described his nagging wife—HIS "BITTER" HALF

135. **Jumbles:** PEONY BOOTY ENDURE SIMILE
Answer: What the poet did when he bought a house—"ODE" ON IT

136. **Jumbles:** METAL ABATE OUTLAW CIPHER
Answer: Experienced by the corpulent diner at the end of a long buffet line—A "WAIT" PROBLEM

137. **Jumbles:** DADDY CREEL MAMMAL BELONG
Answer: What the bill for the skier's injuries amounted to—AN ARM AND A LEG

138. **Jumbles:** COUPE OWING UPWARD WHINNY
Answer: When the racing pigeons neared the finish line, it was—DOWN TO THE WIRE

139. **Jumbles:** AHEAD FAMED UNCURL MINGLE
Answer: What the frugal shopper did when she bought new outfits—"FIGURED"

140. **Jumbles:** DICED MURKY DEFACE MUFFIN
Answer: When the bank robber saw his wanted poster, he said he was—"FRAMED"

141. **Jumbles:** ELEGY SCARF COLUMN BEAGLE
Answer: What the museum visitors considered the famous sculptures—"MARBLE-OUS"

142. **Jumbles:** GUEST DAUNT MOBILE HANSOM
Answer: When the cleaner's presser was late, the owner was—STEAMING, MAD

143. **Jumbles:** DRAMA FORUM BRIDLE MUSEUM
Answer: What the coach did when the player fumbled—MUMBLED

144. **Jumbles:** GROUP PANIC DONKEY HAMPER
Answer: They picked the dog with the wagging tail and had a—HAPPY "ENDING"

145. **Jumbles:** DECAY FLOOD NORMAL EASILY
Answer: What the hardworking baker did—"LOAFED" ALL DAY

146. **Jumbles:** FUROR DRYLY NEWEST UPHELD
Answer: Can be heard with false teeth—TRUE WORDS

147. **Jumbles:** BOWER UNCAP SUPERB JARGON
Answer: What the driver did in the demolition race—A "BANG UP" JOB

186

148. **Jumbles:** POKED LEAVE PYTHON UNLIKE
Answer: When the new prison guard went on duty, he was—"KEYED" UP

149. **Jumbles:** PERKY MAIZE CEMENT TRUSTY
Answer: What the cosmetology student faced when she missed the exam—A "MAKEUP" TEST

150. **Jumbles:** FEINT IRONY PACKET THWART
Answer: When the runner decided to become a novelist, he was on—THE "WRITE" TRACK

151. **Jumbles:** BILGE TASTY WHEEZE DREDGE
Answer: What the forecaster did when the strong storm approached—"WEATHERED" IT

152. **Jumbles:** VOCAL STOOP PATTER HUMBLE
Answer: When the astronauts found the diner on the moon, they said it lacked—"ATMOSPHERE"

153. **Jumbles:** TULIP BLAZE NATURE THEORY
Answer: A good way to get Mom to make their favorite cookies—"BUTTER" HER UP

154. **Jumbles:** BAGGY OUTDO SCRIBE HERALD
Answer: Why the spy talked funny—HE HAD A "CODE"

155. **Jumbles:** SPURN VENOM FICKLE DISMAY
Answer: What the mosquitoes turned into when they spotted the beach party—SKIN DIVERS

156. **Jumbles:** PLAIT ENJOY SCENIC PAGODA
Answer: What the ballerinas did at the audition—"TOED" THE LINE

157. **Jumbles:** GUILE LUNGE KNIGHT AIRWAY
Answer: When the sailors retrieved the ship's bell, it was—"RINGING" WET

158. **Jumbles:** DEMON LOONY BRONCO FACIAL
Answer: Lack of alimony can result in this—ACRIMONY

159. **Jumbles:** GRIEF ADAGE MODISH DEMISE
Answer: What the waitress did to the short order cook—"EGGED" HIM ON

160. **Jumbles:** WHISK POKER WEEVIL PLURAL
Answer: An important exercise for a dieter—WILL POWER

161. **Jumbles:** THIRTY POUNCE OPPOSE BLOUSE COSTLY PAYOFF
Answer: When the doorman was arrested, the detective said it was an—OPEN AND SHUT CASE

162. **Jumbles:** EMBRYO FORGET DEMISE MUSCLE FELLOW AMPERE
Answer: What the reporter demanded when the ironing piled up—FREEDOM OF THE "PRESS"

163. **Jumbles:** CAMPER MUSLIN ASTHMA GENIUS MUFFLE JOVIAL
Answer: The well-mannered counterfeiter gave the bank teller a—FALSE "IMPRESSION"

164. **Jumbles:** TOFFEE MARMOT SEXTON POUNCE ADVICE SLOUCH
Answer: When the hostess baked her own bread for the party, it—ROSE TO THE OCCASION

165. **Jumbles:** CHORUS GENIUS DEPICT ATTACH DULCET THIRTY
Answer: What the hunters did in the swirling river—"SHOT" THE RAPIDS

166. **Jumbles:** HYBRID OPPOSE TURTLE NUMBED MAMMAL FONDLY
Answer: How the newsman described the prison uprising—"PEN-DEMONIUM"

167. **Jumbles:** POCKET JOVIAL TONGUE EMBARK COSTLY POORLY
Answer: Why the chefs couldn't make a good soup—TOO MANY KOOKS

168. **Jumbles:** DAWNED TAUGHT SUBTLY SATIRE MATRON VORTEX
Answer: What she considered the skin doctor's bill—A RASH "STATEMENT"

169. **Jumbles:** BECOME HELIUM EVOLVE FORMAT UNSOLD CUDDLE
Answer: When the fashion plate went shopping, she was—"CLOTHES" MINDED

170. **Jumbles:** HUNGRY LEVITY MARVEL HUMBLE DEFACE PAUNCH
Answer: What the conductor did when the champ rode the train—GAVE HIM A "PUNCH"

171. **Jumbles:** BARROW CARBON LICHEN ORPHAN FERVID SONATA
Answer: When the tree cutter was promoted, he had—HIS OWN "BRANCH"

172. **Jumbles:** GRASSY DREDGE FICKLE PESTLE MODIFY FETISH
Answer: What he considered the optometrist's office—A SITE FOR SORE EYES

173. **Jumbles:** MOTION VASSAL OUTCRY CARNAL FLAXEN PULPIT
Answer: When record players first appeared, they were—"REVOLUTIONARY"

174. **Jumbles:** JAUNTY FLORAL EMBODY DRAGON MAGNUM NIPPLE
Answer: When the sleep therapist asked her out, she said—YOU'RE "DREAMING"

175. **Jumbles:** VARIED PILLAR CORRAL FERVOR PREFER BELFRY
Answer: What the directors gave the company president's plan—"BORED" APPROVAL

176. **Jumbles:** EMPIRE BECAME WHINNY SHAKEN NICELY FORGOT
Answer: When the married mimes left for work, they—WEREN'T SPEAKING

177. **Jumbles:** MUSTER TARTAR CAVORT BICEPS HOMAGE FAUCET
Answer: A good way to climb the ladder of success—START AT THE BOTTOM

178. **Jumbles:** PREFIX DRUDGE MISHAP BREACH MYSELF RUBBER
Answer: The beauty queen turned into this when she addressed the crowd—A "FIGURE" OF SPEECH

179. **Jumbles:** PIRATE GOODLY AUTUMN KNIGHT IMPORT LEGUME
Answer: When the hostess served cocktails, the crochet club became a—"TIGHT" KNIT GROUP

180. **Jumbles:** NEPHEW ENTICE PALLID DONKEY DISOWN EXHALE
Answer: The strikeout artist went into sales because he—KNEW HOW TO "PITCH"

Need More Jumbles®?

Order any of these books through your bookseller or call Triumph Books toll-free at 800-335-5323.